4.2-80

THE ISLANDS SERIES

THE ÅLAND ISLANDS

THE ISLANDS SERIES

published
†Achill
†Alderney
†The Aran Islands
  The Isle of Arran
  The Island of Bute
*Canary Islands: Fuerteventura
*Cape Breton Island
*Corsica
*Cyprus
*Dominica
*The Falkland Islands
†Gotland
*Grand Bahama
†Harris and Lewis
†The Isle of Mull
  Lundy

  The Maltese Islands
*Mauritius
†Orkney
*Puerto Rico
  Ryukyu
  St Kilda and Other Hebridean
    Islands
*The Seychelles
†Shetland
*Sicily
*Singapore
†Skye
*The Solomon Islands
*Tasmania
†Uists and Barra
*Vancouver Island

in preparation
  Bermuda
  Crete
  Fiji
  Greenland
  Guernsey

  Minorca
  St Helena
  Sardinia
  Isles of Scilly
  Tobago

* Published in the United States by Stackpole
† Published in the United States by David & Charles Inc
The series is distributed in Australia by Wren Publishing Pty Ltd Melbourne

THE ÅLAND ISLANDS

by W. R. MEAD and S. H. JAATINEN

DAVID & CHARLES

NEWTON ABBOT LONDON NORTH POMFRET (VT) VANCOUVER

ISBN 0 7153 6734 X

The capital of Finland, Helsinki, is used in
this form throughout the book as it is the
familiar English use. The Swedish form is
Helsingfors.

Set in 11 on 13 point Baskerville
and printed in Great Britain
by Latimer Trend & Company Ltd Plymouth
for David & Charles (Holdings) Limited
South Devon House Newton Abbot Devon

Published in the United States of America
by David & Charles Inc
North Pomfret Vermont 05053 USA

Published in Canada
by Douglas David & Charles Limited
3645 McKechnie Drive West Vancouver BC

CONTENTS

page

1   Introducing Åland   11

2   The Genesis of Åland   26

3   The Ways of the Weather   39

4   Garden of the Northern Hesperides   48

5   The Development of Society and Economy   63

6   A Crossroads of the Baltic   92

7   Life Ashore   112

8   Life Afloat   138

9   The Fortunate Isles   158

    Afterword   172

    Bibliography   174

    Index   179

ILLUSTRATIONS

PLATES   *page*

Wall painting from Finström church   17

Taxation map   17

Fortress of Kastelholm   18

Fortress of Bomarsund   18

An Åland farmhouse   35

An Ålandic fisherman   35

The island setting of Simskäla   36

Sellskär in the outer archipelago (*Rainer Johansson*)   53

The inner archipelago   54

Käringsund   54

Ytternäs in Jomala (*Reino Kalliola*)   71

Country museum at Kastelholm   71

Fortress of Kastelholm (*Volker von Bonin*)   72

Mariehamn town hall (*Ralf Rostén*)   89

Mariehamn main shopping street (*Ralf Rostén*)   89

The church at Finström (*Tourist Office of Åland, Mariehamn*)   90

Logging operations (*Tourist Office of Åland, Mariehamn*)   90

Korrvik harbour   107

Unloading Baltic herring   107

Passage through winter skerries   108

View of the *Pommern* (*Ralf Rostén*)   108

ILLUSTRATIONS

page

A winter car ferry 125
The *Skärgårdsfärjan,* a small car ferry 126
West harbour of Mariehamn (*Ralf Rostén*) 126
Midsummer Eve: traditional maypole (*Ralf Rostén*) 143
Fiftieth anniversary of the autonomy of Åland 143
Maritime Museum at Mariehamn (*Ralf Rostén*) 144
Pike fishing (*Ralf Rostén*) 144

MAPS AND DIAGRAMS

page

The Åland Islands in their Baltic setting 10
The parishes of the province of Åland 20
The physical evolution of the Åland archipelago 27
Rock names of the Åland skerries 34
The climate of Mariehamn 42
A phenological diagram for Åland mainland 44
An ecological traverse through Åland mainland 49
Components of a nineteenth-century Åland homestead 82
Contemporary land use on the main island of
Kumlinge parish 115
The historic post route from Sweden to Finland 124
Motor-bus and ferry communications, 1973 124
The changing distribution of population and
employment 131
Population pyramids for sample parishes, 1970, with a
pyramid for 1750 132
The 'Great Grain Race', 1935 150
The growth of the tourist trade 166

ILLUSTRATIONS

We wish to thank the following for permission to use illustrations: The Finnish Foreign Ministry, The National Museum of Finland, Atenaeum, Lantmäteristyrelsen, The Tourist Office of Åland, Professor Reino Kalliola and Mr Carl-Eric Södergårdh.

The maps and diagrams were prepared by Mr Kenneth Wass, of the Cartography Unit in the Department of Geography at University College London.

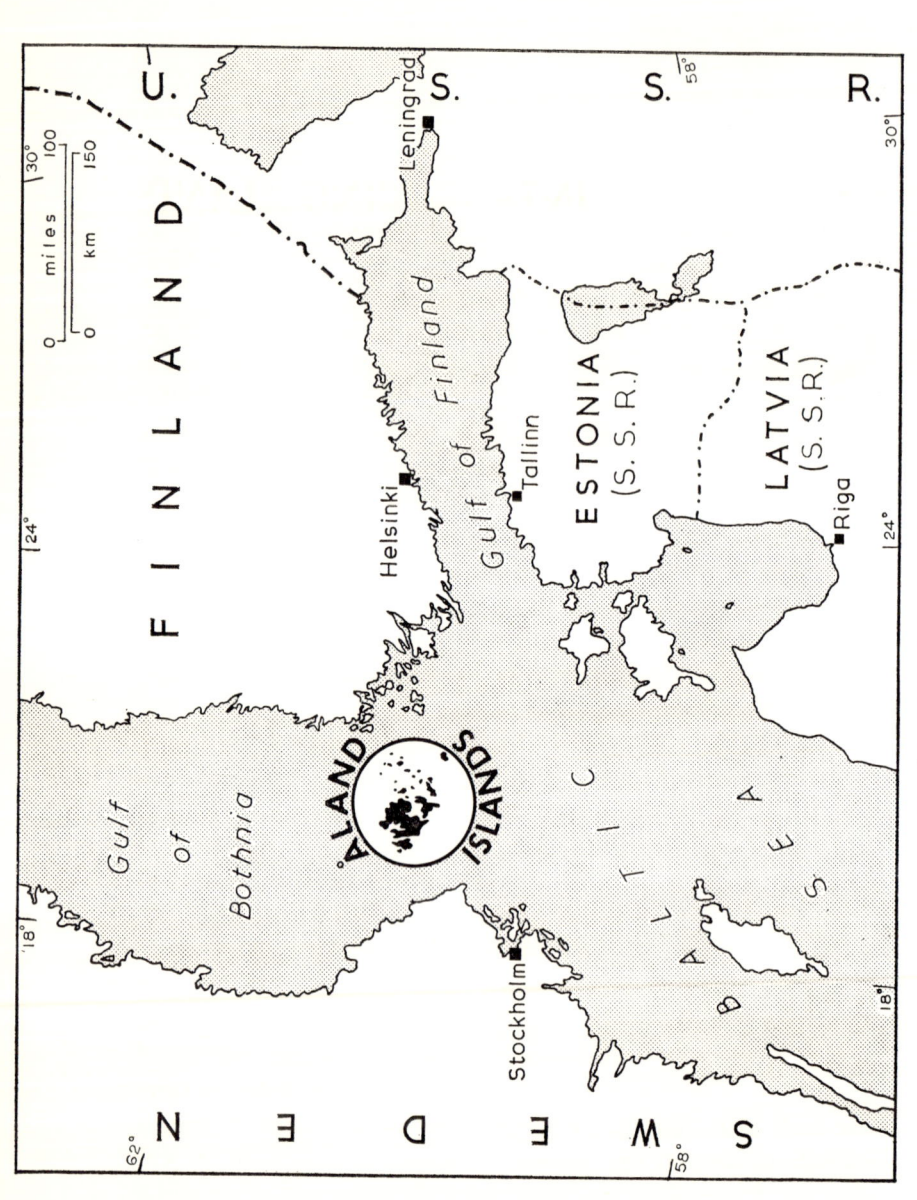

The Åland Islands in their Baltic setting

1 INTRODUCING ÅLAND

SCANDINAVIA has two faces: its western face looks to the outer ocean—the Atlantic; its eastern face looks to an inner sea—the Baltic. Both the Atlantic coast and the Baltic coast are richly islanded. The island clusters are called *skärgårdar* (*skärgård*, in the singular). Nowhere in the world is there a concentration of islands quite the same as that in the central Baltic. Daniel Defoe, in a text to an atlas published in 1723, described the area as 'differing from all the rest of the world for rocks and little rocky islands'. Among the many archipelagos in the Baltic, none has clearer identity than the Åland Islands (Ahvenanmaa, in Finnish). Åland lies midway between Stockholm archipelago and the archipelago of Åbo (Turun saaristo, in Finnish). To the west, Åland is separated from the outermost skerries of Sweden by the Åland Sea (Ålands hav, as the Ålanders know it). East of Åland, the island galaxies thin out and a natural break occurs in Skiftet, a channel ten or more kilometres wide, beyond which lie the islands of Åboland.

Most travellers approach Åland across the sea from the west. It was the way followed by many of its earliest settlers; it was the crossing established in the days of post boat and diligence, and it is the route confirmed by the present-day shuttle of ferry boats. The Åland Sea, some 40km of open water, is tideless and, although capricious by reputation, is rarely rough enough to disturb the ferries. In winter it is frequently ice-covered. The modern traveller, unless he is a friend of a yachtsman, will take his pick of the variety of vessels that depart daily from the harbour of Stockholm or from one of its outports. The ferries are extravagant in appointment and almost aggressive in appearance. They throb with life, are lavish in restaurants and duty-free shops and, by Swedish standards, offer such a cheap and cheerful experience that Stockholmers can scarcely afford to stay at home. Åland's western outposts are only a journey of several hours from the Swedish capital.

The islands lie low on the water and first appear as no more than a mirage—floating in the sky before they settle on the surface of the sea. They announce themselves discreetly—their broken rim of granite coppery red on a bright day, capped by the dark green line of the forest. They are protected by a girdle of rocky islets and reefs, through the treacherous channels of which the ferry twists and turns, sensitive to every seamark, buoy, beacon and lighthouse. The barren reefs of the outer islands are unoccupied save by sea birds and the occasional bleakly perched home of a pilot. Such an introduction to Åland makes the visitor feel that it was rightly named for, etymologically, Åland is 'the land belonging to the sea'. Beyond the 'sheres', as eighteenth-century British mariners used to call such skerries, the ship rounds the wooded promontory and enters the home stretch to the waterfront of Mariehamn, provincial capital of the islands.

Mariehamn (Maarianhamina, in Finnish) is not much more than a hundred years old, and appears much larger than its population of 9,000 suggests. An extensive quay, landscaped into the low bluff up which Mariehamn climbs on its seaward side, receives the steady procession of ferries. Not much of the town can be seen from the multiple decks of the ferry boats, but from the top of the nearby water tower there is a good bird's-eye view of its setting. Its loose chequerboard plan of roads is laid over a fairly rocky peninsula several kilometres wide. In summer, Mariehamn is a green and leafy place—even leafier than the average Middle Western American county town, the layout of which it closely resembles. Avenues of linden, birch and aspen open to modest parks which boast lithe young oaks and larches and which are backed by gardens where flowering shrubs and apple trees flourish. The granite slopes on which the newer suburbs have developed retain many of their pines. The waters on the eastern side of the peninsula—broader but shallower than those on the western side—are alive with pleasure boats. Pastel-shaded clapboard houses, white-painted blocks of flats and balconied hotels break through the intervening green. Below the water tower, yachts anchor close to the square-rigger *Pommern*, a carefully restored museum ship. On the adjacent terrace is a monument which symbolises Åland in its inscription: *Vår väg är havet*—our way lies seaward.

The monument is at the entrance to Mariehamn's broadest boulevard, along which are strung administrative buildings, consulates and hotels, an old people's home, the museum and the Lutheran church—all in garden settings. The business area is at its eastern end and is concentrated along one street. The same cars seem to pass continuously up and down it, the same visitors to throng it constantly. In the summer season, there must be twenty or thirty visitors for every Ålander and all equally laden with shopping bags. The crowd is distinctively Scandinavian—blond, sunburnt, brightly dressed. Swedish is the language used by almost everybody. The precincts of central Mariehamn, and especially its main street, are in process of lively transformation. The traditional wooden dwellings, built around a central *gård* or yard, secure upon the solid granite blocks of their basements, tarred roofs above the fretwork decoration of their clapboarding, are being torn down. They are being replaced by the functional cubic structures that are common to all of Finland—clean, economic but characterless. As a result, people say that Mariehamn is no longer Ålandic in atmosphere. Nevertheless, it remains the gateway to Åland and those who enjoy the picturesque rather than the practical can speedily pass through it.

THE ÅLAND ISLANDS

THE SETTING OF THE ISLANDS

Mariehamn is on Fasta Åland, mainland Åland, the largest island. Although mainland Åland accounts for two-thirds of the 1,426sq km of the total land area of the archipelago, it is only one among thousands of islands. Encyclopaedias ascribe to Åland no fewer than 6,500 islands, and up to 9,000 have been identified. About seventy are permanently occupied, but many others are inhabited seasonally. In some respects the most remarkable island is the most remote. It is Märket, on which Åland shares a land boundary with Sweden, for it lies athwart the international boundary that divides the territorial waters of Sweden and Finland.

The Åland Islands are a part of the low-lying and much fragmented granite area of northern Europe that stretches from Sweden to the White Sea shores. Its heavily eroded surface is littered with boulders, gravels and sands deposited by the retreating Quaternary ice sheet. From these deposits, resorted by the waves and currents of post-glacial seas, Åland—like most of Fennoscandia—has emerged during the last 10,000 years. Physically, therefore, Åland differs little from the neighbouring island groups, but it rises to altitudes of 130m on its northern flanks and commands broader vistas from them than are obtainable from the heights of the Swedish and Finnish archipelagos. In addition, it rejoices in a remarkably varied flora. Not only is it Finland's richest floristic province, but, as a result of the intimate variety of local land forms, pronounced contrasts in vegetation occur in close juxtaposition. 'The flowery isles of a dream' was the epithet applied to it by the English traveller Amelia Heber in 1805. Insect and bird life are correspondingly abundant; so, too, is the variety of cultivated plants.

But in a European context, such features are relative. The ameliorating influence of the sea on the climate of Åland has powerful rivals in high latitude and a continental setting. From December until April, the character and appearance of the Åland Islands are completely transformed—fit setting only for a temple to Odin is the view of a French historian. In all but the mildest winters, Åland becomes a part of the mainland. Snow covers its surface and the distinguishing vegetational mantle is hidden. Ice covers most of its territorial waters—all of them in hard winters. In 1799 Edward Clarke dubbed it a 'hyperborean Hades'. The personality of Åland is rooted partly in these powerful seasonal contrasts and in its corresponding ecological sensitivity. Its character cannot be understood from a summer visit.

Given this setting, with its attendant constraints, the individuality of Åland is an expression firstly of its people and what they have done with their island home, secondly of its neighbours and how they have impinged upon it. Åland has been settled for over 5,000 years. Fish, fowl and flesh (from the seal in the sea to the elk on the land) drew hunters and settlers at a relatively early stage in the occupation of the Scandinavian territory. By the standards of mainland western Europe, Åland is not rich in antiquities; but by Scandinavian criteria the countryside of Åland has the feel of long occupation. There are high level rocky caverns occupied at intervals since the Finnish Stone Age and sources of myth and legend. There are tumuli by the thousand, boat grave sites, Dark Age hill forts, formidable medieval churches and some resistant military ruins. While Åland has not yielded pirate gold, it has produced considerable treasure trove. Farmstead, field and forest lot—strung together by winding roads and tracks, and long occupied by owner-farmers—have a mature air. Farm name and family name are often one and the same, and have been for generations. Farmhouses are commodious; farm buildings, capacious. But there are few old domestic buildings. As with the rest of Scandinavia, timber has been the principal constructional material. It is easily destroyed by fire; it also rots. Comparatively speaking, Åland has probably always looked well cared for. Generations of travellers have commented on the neatness of its farmsteads. It remains affectionately tended, exuding a pride of possession at both the personal and the community level.

THE PATRIMONY OF THE ISLANDERS

The patrimony of the Ålanders is divided into fifteen parishes, each of which has its own peculiar qualities. Eight of them— Finström, Geta, Hammarland, Jomala, Lemland, Lumparland, Saltvik and Sund—have their churches on the main island. To the west, a bridge links the nearby island parish of Eckerö. Vårdö is its complement on the eastern side of Fasta Åland. More far flung are Föglö, Sottunga and Kumlinge; remotest of all are Kökar and Brändö. Each of these parishes has its own congeries of islands, so that its boundaries are traced through water rather than through land. So, too, are most of the networks of property boundaries which have been increasingly sharpened and refined as settlement pushed to the limits of inhabitable land. The islands beyond the core of the parish— the last to be occupied permanently and, not unusually, the first to be abandoned—are in some respects the quintessence of Åland. They have supported the ultimate in isolated settlement, remote from the amenity and authority of the church village, distant even from the secondary hamlets. Their inhabitants, usually the last to receive the impulse of new ideas, have often been the last to retain the residue of custom and tradition (which folklorist and social historian have gleaned and winnowed for posterity). Each family settlement on the outer isles has been a near law unto itself—knowing the detail of its territory like the lines on the palm of its patriarch's hand; pressing into service the skerries as collecting grounds, hunting lands, summer grazings or sites for fishing cabins; baptising them with the names of men when the names of nature were exhausted. Here, above all, were acquired by a succession of

16

Page 17   (above) A wall painting from Finström church illustrating a medieval *kogge* or trading vessel; (below) taxation map from *Åland och Sund Chartebok* by Hans Hansson, 1650

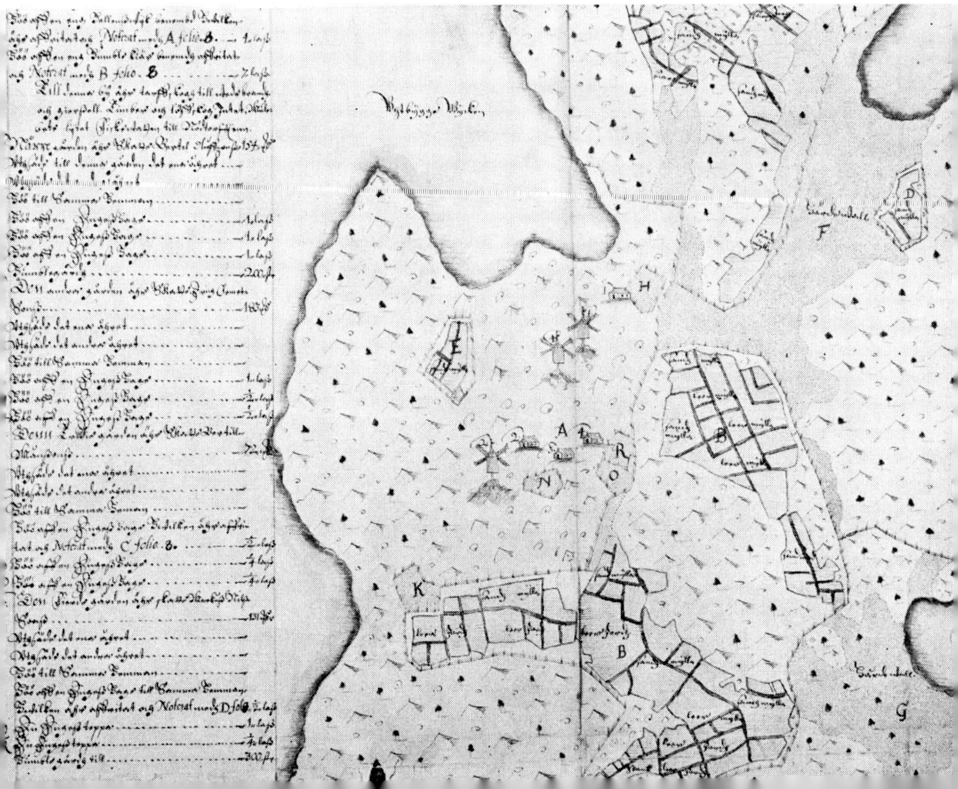

Page 18 (*above*) Fortress of Kastelholm as depicted in Eric Dahlberg's *Suecia Antiqua et Hodierna, 1691–1716*; (*below*) Fortress of Bomarsund as it was in 1854. A woodcut from *Illustrated London News*

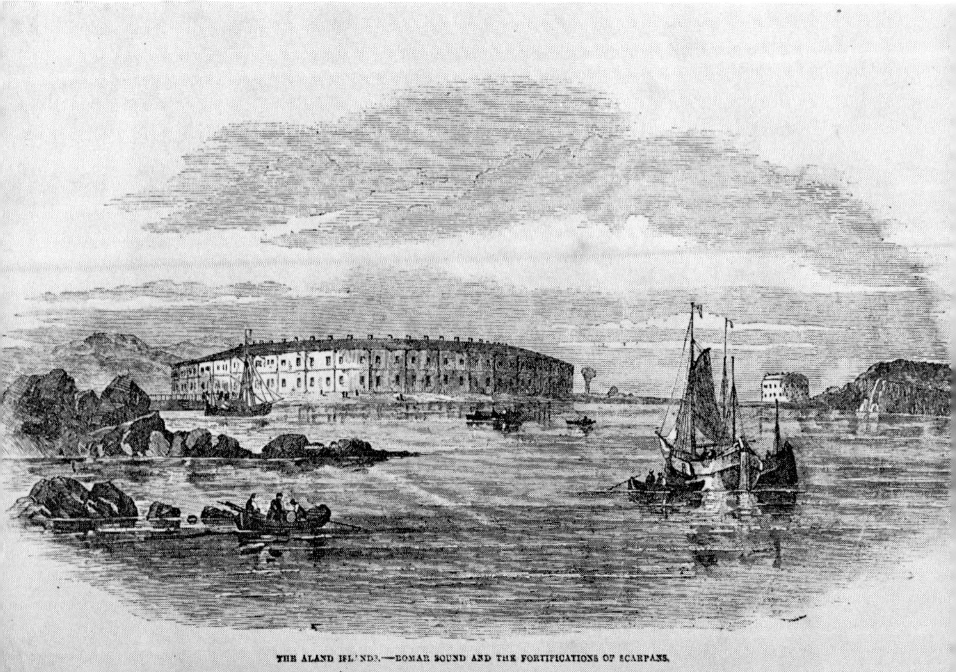

THE ÅLAND ISL'ND?.—BOMAR SOUND AND THE FORTIFICATIONS OF SCARPANS.

generations the handful of lowly accomplishments and skills that enabled body and soul to be kept together, and the cunning in the face of natural hazard that permitted only the very successful or the most fortunate to survive. The doctrines of natural selection and geographical determinism may be dead, but it is difficult to deny that at least for some Ålanders some of the qualities of independent outlook and individuality owe their origins to this kind of upbringing.

Pride of possession and independence of outlook lie partly behind the fact that Åland is a would-be nation in miniature. Åland was a part of the Swedish kingdom from the eleventh century until 1809. Thereafter, it was a province of the Grand Duchy of Finland. Åland remains a county of the Republic of Finland, but it has autonomous status. The 20,000 Ålanders (*Ålänningar*, as they call themselves) are almost entirely Swedish-speaking; and Finland is a state where 94 per cent of the population is Finnish-speaking. Ålanders originated principally from the Swedish mainland, though on archaeological evidence alone the islands seem to have experienced a fair admixture of people. In any case, they are sensitive to their distinctive position, maintaining a cool detachment from Finland but no longer seeking reunion with Sweden. They constitute a quasi-sea state, jealous of what they have made out of their limited opportunities and of the apparent independence that they derive from their enterprise. 'The inhabitant of Åland is always proud of his country. When you ask him if he is a Swede or a Finn, he replies in a firm voice and lifting up his head says that he is an Ålander.' Léouzon le Duc's observation from five generations ago suggests that the feeling of independence is of long standing.

Not surprisingly, the attitude of the Ålanders to the outer world is ambivalent, expressing itself in many ways. For example, Ålanders are accustomed to broad maritime horizons and are born of ancestors bred to the seven seas; but ashore they are inclined to retreat behind their bosky gardens and

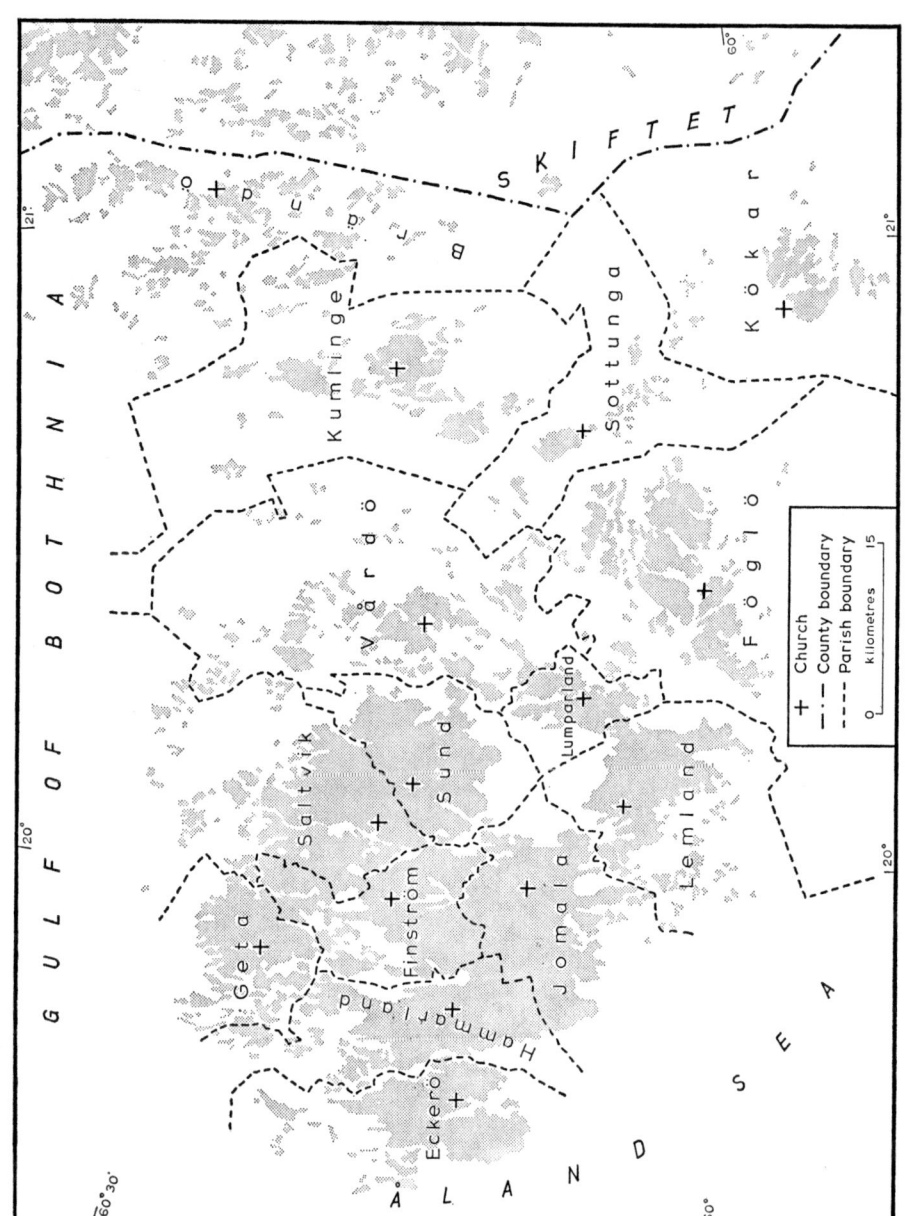

The parishes of the province of Åland

GULF OF BOTHNIA

SKIFTET

Brändö

Kumlinge

Kökar

Sottunga

Vårdö

Föglö

Saltvik

Sund

Lumparland

Geta

Finström

Jomala

Lemland

Hammarland

Eckerö

ÅLAND SEA

Church +
County boundary —·—·—
Parish boundary ------

0   kilometres   15

verandahs. An Ålander's home is very much his castle. Again, few Baltic communities have a closer physical association with the Eastsea (Östersjön, as they call it) than the Ålanders. Yet they adopt an almost cavalier spirit of detachment from its geopolitical realities. For Åland occupies a central position in the Baltic arena as well as providing the historical route between Sweden and Finland. Its location has resulted in unavoidable involvement in every war which has affected control of the Baltic Sea. Before granite block was heaved upon granite block to build the fortress of Kastelholm on Åland mainland in the late fourteenth century, there had already been a stockaded wooden fort. Kastelholm, first sign of Sweden's offensive thrust to the east, was later converted into its last defensive outwork. And when Kastelholm ceased to be Åland's focus, the Russian fortress at Bomarsund, residence of a poliglot army of several thousands, emerged as the westernmost of Russia's strong points. Åland, held in the balance of Baltic political systems, has been pressurised, occupied, fortified, neutralised, demilitarised. The Ålanders, unable to resist external authority, have nevertheless contrived to persist in spite of it. Sometimes they have fled before invaders (as on the occasion when Russians have overrun the archipelago); sometimes they have stood apart from the belligerents (as during the Crimean War); sometimes they have been a shuttlecock in diplomatic manoeuvres (as in 1914 18 and 1939–44). When the League of Nations commission eventually sought their political wishes by referendum in 1920, their vote for reunion with Sweden was disregarded. It is scarcely surprising that they should view international affairs with scepticism.

Ambivalence has also characterised their attitude to those who have used the historic Åland post route in transit between Sweden and Finland. Post boat, post chaise, post sleigh, post house and ferry constituted the components in a critical system of communication which persisted until the 1870s. The Ålanders supplied the services to all whose business carried them along

21

the most difficult part of the route between Stockholm and St Petersburg—monarch and ambassador, soldier and priest, civil servant and merchant. Monarchy left its monograms— Peter the Great's name is chiselled on a rock flank in Ledskär; those of Gustav III and Gustaf Adolf IV are recorded on the rock face at Brakholm in Föglö and Södö in Sottunga respectively. Carl Linnaeus scribbled perfunctory notes about Åland. From the later eighteenth century onwards, a variety of European travellers have left full accounts of their journeys through the isles. Signildsskär—little Åland beyond Åland, as it might be called—was the most westerly island group for those who left their homeland to seek refuge in Sweden. Adolf Erik Nordenskiöld, leaving Finland for exile, wrote of it as his 'fatherland's forefinger—always pointing the way to the older brother, Sweden'.

The trickle of travellers of a century ago has become a flood of tourists whose summer tide swamps the main island for several weeks on end. More than a million visitors set foot on Åland each year. They are neither easily controlled nor contained, though they are welcomed for the substantial contribution that they make to the island's economy. Indeed, on grounds of protection alone, Ålanders must adopt a mental if not physical detachment from them. In the face of the changing nature of this seasonal migration, Ålanders have also had to protect their territory in another way. The archipelago offers ideal sites for camping and summer residence. Furthermore, as farmsteads and fishermen's cabins are abandoned, they are coveted for conversion by those from the more crowded shores of the Baltic. It has been necessary to refer increasingly to Åland's constitutional provision for the right of pre-emption on every occasion when offers to purchase land in the archipelago are made by outsiders. *Noli me tangere* is a motto which, in all senses of the word, might be adopted by the islands.

INTRODUCING ÅLAND

The particular identity of Åland is a blend of the traditional and the contemporary. Traditionally, it has its strongest expression in the farming and fishing communities. In its contemporary expression, Åland is most assertive in the provincial capital of Mariehamn. Created in 1861 and well located on the south of the main island, Mariehamn was named after the Russian empress Maria, wife of Alexander II. As the official trading centre of the island, it has exerted a steady pull, and migration to it has become increasingly strong. In it, Åland is most articulate. Mariehamn had had its own newspaper since 1891. Its sixty-year-old lyceum centralises secondary education in the islands; its navigation school provides formal training for its mariners. Those who live in and around it have somehow to sustain the full range of services and amenities expected of a minor boom town. There are factories for processing farm products, a provincial hospital, an electricity station and an airport. Over the administrative offices of the provincial capital, where the *Landsting* celebrated the fiftieth anniversary of its foundation in 1972, flies the red, yellow and blue flag of Åland. It is a variation of the old Swedish flag and was conceded to the province on the occasion of a presidential visit in 1955. As with the Faeroe Islands, Åland sends a delegate to meetings of the Nordic Council. It is paradoxical that the outward expressions of its identity are most manifest at a time when the island community, both socially and economically, is more closely integrated with Finland and Sweden than ever before.

Above all, Åland has expressed itself on the sea. For C. A. Cederborg, the Ålander was 'an amphibious small-holder'. He has always been a fisherman and boatbuilder, combining life on land and life at sea. The humble climax of that combination was reached a hundred years ago at which time most Ålanders

23

participated in maritime trading. 'A coffee pot and a share in a trading vessel are reckoned among the necessities of life', a correspondent wrote from Åland in 1875. Today, Åland is bound to the outer world by a ceaseless shuttle of ferries which winter ice may delay but may no longer allay. About a third of Finland's 1·6 million tons of merchant shipping are registered in Mariehamn, giving to the Ålanders a *per capita* tonnage higher than that of the Norwegians. These ships, invisible sources of income for the island's purse, rarely, if ever, appear in home waters. Former money-spinners lie at anchor in the western roadsteads of Mariehamn—tankers and cargo vessels waiting for the scrap yard or for better times, as well as the four-master, *Pommern*, last of the sailing fleet. In summer, pleasure craft take possession—plastic, plywood and fibreglass propelled by outboard motors; yachts, both dignified and impudent. Grey coastguard cutters link the innumerable lighthouses, provide emergency services for summer boatmen and endeavour to patrol well-nigh unpatrollable waters against the age-old practice of smuggling. The old jingle that Zachris Topelius applied to Åland still holds:

> *Och usel kallas här den man*
> *Som ej sitt segel sköta kan*

(And useless they call a man here if he cannot manage his sail boat.)

From the natural features it has inherited and the human features it has acquired, the personality of Åland has been compounded. To sum up—and to anticipate. The archipelago of Åland is a gift of the Baltic. Its primeval rocks, rounded by ice, lifted above post-glacial seas, endowed with relatively rich if scanty soils, shaped by wave (if not scoured by tide), are played upon by the summer whims and winter asperities of a climate of pronounced contrasts, the hardships of which have not infrequently been greater in the past than in the present.

By the standards of the inner Baltic and in a Finnish context, the Åland Islands are virtual gardens of the Hesperides. Settlers were early attracted to them and have nurtured in them a fisher-farming community which, since records have been kept, has been fostered by church and state. Åland is at the crossroads of the Baltic—the western approaches to Finland or the eastern springboard to metropolitan Sweden, according to the point of view. Its centrality, concentrating international attention upon it, has regularly affected the fortunes of its people whose attitudes are dominated by the dispersion of their settlement and interests.

The Åland Islands could well adopt the motif of Margaret of Austria's monumental shrine to Philibert le Beau at Bourg en Bresse—*Fortune, Misfortune, Fortune.* In this ecologically and politically sensitive environment, even minor swings in the pendulum can have major consequences. Fortune favours Åland today, but in gaining the products of the material world that lie on its doorstep it could suffer the misfortune of losing its natural identity. The new accessibility and new mobility that it experiences have alerted planners and conservationists alike. With their long record of detachment, Ålanders should therefore be capable of selecting those opportunities in the present situation that favour their fortune and to reject the elements that could lead to misfortune in their island community.

2　THE GENESIS OF ÅLAND

ÅLAND is a part of the great Fennoscandian or Baltic Shield, a land mass which dates from earliest geological times. The Shield is composed principally of granites, gneisses, gabbros and other crystalline rocks—some of the most resistant as well as oldest rocks in the world. The structure of the Shield is very complex and the present-day surface, a low-lying peneplain, is but the core of what were once mountain ranges. Here and there into the older primary rocks, intrusions of younger and more homogenous granites have occurred. The greater part of the bedrock of Åland consists of such an intrusion, which dominates mainland Åland and the eastern islands (eg Vårdö); it is called in Finnish, *rapakivi* and in Swedish, *självfrätsten*. The rock is sufficiently distinctive for it to have commanded the attention of naturalists at an early stage in the history of their science. For Carl Linnaeus, it was 'Åland stone'; for nineteenth-century British geologists, 'rotten granite'; for the perceptive Zachris Topelius, 'a caricature of granite'. The *rapakivi* area in Åland covers about 4,000sq km. Its boundary to the east is sharp; while to the west, the *rapakivi* layer thins out gradually. In colour, the *rapakivi* granite ranges from dark red through reddish brown to brown. On sunny days, it provides a bright rim along the shoreline. In composition, it consists of potassium felspar ovoids (about 1–2cm in diameter and thinly covered with sodium felspar) embedded in a mass of quartzes, felspars and micas, with hornblende and biotite as

26

TIME SCALE	EVOLUTION	CLIMATE — Phase	Precipitation change	Temp. change	SEA LEVEL (metres)	HISTORICAL DIVISIONS
A.D. +2000		SUB ATLANTIC			0+	
+1000	POST GLACIAL — LIMNAEA SEA				10+	MIDDLE AGES
						VIKING
0		"Fimbul winter"			20+	IRON AGE
-1000					30+	BRONZE AGE
-2000		SUB BOREAL			40+	
-3000						STONE AGE (comb ceramic)
B.C. -4000	LITORINA — Highest level of Litorina Sea	ATLANTIC			70+	
-5000	Mastogloa Sea					
-6000		BOREAL			100+	
-7000	YOLDIA SEA / FINI GLACIAL / ANCYLUS LAKE — Echinels Sea		Decrease / Increase	Lower / Higher	140+	
-8000		SUBARCTIC			160+	
-9000	GOTIGLACIAL / BALTIC ICE LAKE — Gyrosigma Sea	COLD & DRY				
-10000	Rhabdonema Sea	RELATIVELY DRY & WARM				

The physical evolution of the Åland archipelago

lesser elements. The chemistry of the granite controls the colour that it adds to the landscape and the distinctive features of its weathering.

The form of the *rapakivi* surface is an expression of its origin. The cooling subsequent to its intrusion into the pre-existing complex of older granites gave rise to a system of fractures which controls present-day relief. In the west, especially in Eckerö and Hammarland, the cooling seems to have taken place more rapidly and has produced a well-marked pattern

27

of horizontal fracturing. In the eastern part of the area, where the *rapakivi* intrusion had its source, cooling seems to have been slower. The orientation of the fractures, which run partly in a north-west direction, is less uniform. The result for the landscape is that the granite is split into great cube-shaped blocks, often with steeply sloping sides. They give to the relief a more dramatic quality than is found in other parts of the islands— Wolf's Glen rather than Dingley Dell, to use an early nineteenth-century metaphor. The *rapakivi* massif has also been affected by later earth movements which have resulted in a steeper northern slope and a gently dipping southern slope. Indeed, the northern face of Åland mainland has an almost scarp-like profile, though the bedding planes produce a step-like form on the ground. These characteristics are repeated in a second area north of the Kyrksund lakes in the parish of Sund. In general, relief is higher and more broken in the eastern and northern parts of the main island than in the western and southern. Eastern Åland has a bedrock older than the *rapakivi*, the relief of which is lower, but more irregular. Its structure displays some unusual features, such as the strikingly circular Ängskärsfjärden in the parish of Brändö, the boundary islands of which give the illusion of the drowned rim of a volcanic cone.

In the course of time, the granites and gneisses of Åland were overlain with younger geological formations, but these have been almost completely eroded. Sandstone boulders from the so-called Jotnian period are a component of the moraines. They are also widely scattered around the coasts of Åland and are presumed to derive from the sandstone area in the bed of the Bothnian Sea to the north. The boulders are red in colour and easily split along their thin layers. Some of the fractures in the granite are also filled with Cambrian sandstone. A second sedimentary rock found in Åland is Silurian limestone, though Roderick Murchison, who conceived the Silurian system, never recorded it when he passed through the islands. The limestone is widely dispersed in the moraine as boulders, which are often curiously weathered. Secondly, there are larger scattered blocks, some of which were formerly of considerable dimensions, though most of them have disappeared as a result of limeburning. Thirdly, and more extensively, the limestone masks the surface of several large tracts of the *rapakivi* area. The largest of these is submerged beneath Lumparen Bay, where, at a depth of 30m, a layer of Silurian limestone and Jotnian sandstone some 50m thick has been deposited on top of the *rapakivi*. Similar circumstances clearly characterise the formations underlying some of Åland's plain-like features in eastern Jomala and in Hammarland. These are all related to the most extensive area of Silurian limestone in the Central Baltic, in Gävle Bay to the north-west of Åland, on the coast of the Swedish mainland. However, neither of these older sedimentary formations has had any significance for the topography or economy of Åland. There is a major break in the geological series between the primary rocks and the most recent deposits of the Quaternary period.

In the early 1950s, a deep shaft was lowered into iron-bearing rocks at Nyhamn, but it has not proved economic to operate the rather low grade ore body. Some mineralogists are optimistic that the shape of Åland's lesser local domes and cupolas indicates the presence of tin; but it seems unlikely that the islands will ever become a lesser Cassiterides.

THE LEGACY OF THE ICE AGE

The Quaternary Ice Age had an extremely powerful influence on Åland. The ice sheet, which advanced over Åland from the north-west and which, it is estimated, had a thickness of 165–175m, brought about a rejuvenation of its relief. Old fractures were cleared of their accumulated debris; old erosion features were given a new form. Fiord-like inlets, such as Verkviken and Karvik, on the north coast of the main island, provide striking illustrations of the effects of glaciation on lines of weakness. Striations on the granite surface bear witness to the direction of movement of ice lobes. The smoothing and polishing work of the ice, locally supported by the action of meltwater, is complemented by the action of the ice in plucking out blocks from the bedrock. In this way, many of the irregularly shaped depressions (known to Ålanders as *hällkar*) have been excavated. Where they lie near to sea level, these rock basins sometimes fill with salt water, sometimes with fresh. They have been described by Alvar Palmgren as 'aquaria of nature's own making' and they provide an unusual environment for lesser organisms. *Roches moutonées*, sharply eroded on their distal side and streamlined on their frontal side, are another legacy of the ice movement. The debris removed as the ice sheet advanced over the Åland area has been widely distributed around the Baltic Sea. Most celebrated of the boulders transported is the so-called Hindenburg block in East Prussia.

In Åland itself, the eroded material deposited by the retreating ice has its most elevated expression in the shape of drumlins and drumlin-like features. A good example is found in Ramsholmen, west of Mariehamn. In Sund and Saltvik especially, *rapakivi* outcrops often have a 'tail' of moraine on their southern sides; these correspond to the familiar Scottish 'crag and tail' features. Ålandic morainic deposits are as a rule very finely ground, almost cement-like.

After the retreat of the ice sheet, the whole of the Åland area lay beneath the sea. The diagram on p 27 gives some idea of the subsequent evolution of the Central Baltic area. The release of meltwaters caused a rapid rise in the sea level during the immediate post-glacial period. The episode is known as the Yoldia Sea phase, after a salt-water mollusc, the shells of which remain in the marine sediments. In the ensuing phase, the Baltic area was temporarily cut off from the outer ocean to form the so-called Ancylus Lake, identified by the remains of a fresh-water mollusc. Subsequently, a breach in the Kattegat area again converted the lake into an area of the outer ocean.

This is commonly known as the Litorina episode in the evolution of the Baltic Sea.

It was during the Ancylus period that the rocky summits in Geta and Saltvik began to emerge from the sea. Land uplift, at about 60cm a century, was at its maximum at the same time. The impressive boulder fields (*stenåkrar*, as they are called in Swedish) found, for instance, on the southern flanks of Orrdalsklint, at about 100m above sea level, belong to this episode. They may be several acres in extent and aligned in ridges. Some consist of rounded boulders, others of angular boulders; the former result from marine abrasion, the latter appear to owe their origins to local rock shattering, perhaps as a consequence of intensified freeze-thaw action in earlier times. Undercutting on Orrdalsklint and Getaberg belongs to the same period.

During the Litorina stage, the level of the sea stood at approximately the 55m contour and with it are associated the first Stone Age remains. They have been recovered from sites on the slopes of Orrdalsklint. The speed of land upheaval slackened at the 30–40m level, at which altitudes extensive sand terraces occur on the southern flanks of the hilly areas of mainland Åland. The sand probably owes its origins to glacial streams that deposited their burdens at the edge of the ice sheet. At lower altitudes, clays are encountered, some of which have the distinctively layered form that are known as varved clays (in Swedish *varv* = layer). Thin layers of sand frequently occur between the clays, while elsewhere clays may be overlain with organic soils which lead to swampy conditions. Relatively extensive clay plains are found on the main island, as in Haga-slätten in Saltvik, Jomala-slätten east of the church village, and the central parts of Hammarland. Elsewhere, land upheaval and deposition have given rise to virtual 'clay' fiords which run inland between the often whale-backed rock ridges. In the skerries, it is possible to detect these features in process of evolution, with the shoreline retreating at the rate of 3–5m a generation. Throughout Fennoscandia, mineral soils suffer considerably from leaching, though the relatively favourable climate of Åland has checked the degree of podsolisation. The lime content of the soils—especially those of the more recently emerged land—is higher than that of most Scandinavian soils.

THE NATURE OF
CONTEMPORARY GEOMORPHOLOGICAL PROCESSES

The continued weathering of the bedrock is clearly visible. The granite surface readily fractures along its bedding planes, yielding rectangular blocks of widely varying dimensions. At the same time, land upheaval continuously retraces the boundary between land and sea and, to a greater or lesser degree, causes rejuvenation of the landscape. The process is much more complex than one of simple and uniform pressure release. Åland may fall within a common isoline so far as the speed of upheaval is concerned, but the precise nature of adjustment can vary from locality to locality. Two points may be noted: first, sedimentation versus erosion as conditioned by vegetation can increase or decrease the speed of shore retreat; secondly, drainage is directly affected, with consequences for the sedimentation process and the entire biotic environment.

In general, the considerable variations in relief over the short distance that characterise Åland make for a relatively well-drained land. Streams are of modest size, but their shallow valleys are liable to seasonal flooding. Areas of marsh and peat are restricted. The most extensive peat-lands occur in the interior of Lemland and along the borders between Jomala and Hammarland parishes. True high mosses are lacking.

The sea works relentlessly on the geomorphology of the shoreline, but its effects are more subdued than along the shores of most countries because of the nature of the littoral. The bedrock is very resistant, so that marine erosion is largely confined to the glacial deposits—the gravel and boulder stretches that are slowly lifted into raised beaches. In some parts of the skerries, where there are islands consisting of fluvio-glacial materials, the land has been entirely refashioned by the sea. Examples are found in the small islands of Sandtuvorna and Ölandet, north of Kökar. Sea ice in winter also plays an important erosive role, especially in boulder transport. The most unusual coastal feature, the so-called Kälskärskannan, is also found in Kökar. Here, marine action has refined the coastal exposures of granite, whose original sculpturing is ascribed to the work of meltwater streams beneath the surface of the Quaternary ice. The sequences of worn-out pot-holes, the chains of kettle holes and the naked mammalated features of the rocks that distinguish Kälskär, produce the effect of nature outdoing art.

SEASCAPE AND LANDSCAPE

Håkan Kulves has written that, in transverse section, 'Åland is a review of geological and geomorphological time'. Åland has been, and remains, on a slowly moving staircase which gradually lifts it higher above the surrounding seas. For this reason, a transverse section is a preview as well as a review of geomorphological time. To follow the edge of the sea is to witness the evidence. Accordingly, the delicate balance between land and water is of the essence of Åland. It is fundamental to its scientific understanding and to its aesthetic appreciation at the macro and micro levels. Ole Eklund has commented that students of the *skärgård* are either captivated by it as a total phenomenon or mesmerised by its detail. Some suffer the pleasurable agony of both reactions. The same comment might be made about the language in which the phenomenon is explained. *Skärgård* lacks a clearly defined etymology. Eirik Hornborg believes that the word originated as a narrow folk concept; *gård* in its everyday sense is simply a fence cast around

33

an area of land. By transference, it becomes a fence of smaller islands (*skär*), paralleling the settled coastland or surrounding a larger island. The vocabulary employed to deal with the components of the archipelago is an abracadabra in its own right.

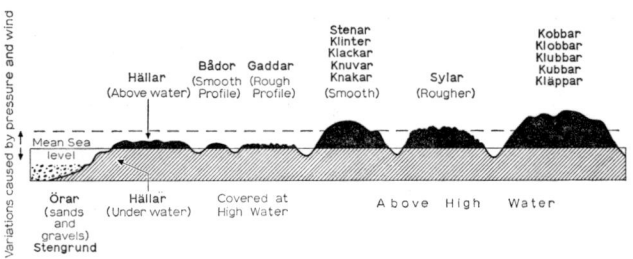

Rock names of the Åland skerries

The traditional names employed for the different zones of the archipelago world are identified in the above diagram. Farthest seaward is Yttre Skärgården, the outer *skärgård* and threshold looking to Skärgårdshavet, the *skärgård* sea. The island components of this zone rejoice in splendidly onomatopoeic nomenclature; some are incorporated in the diagram above. Water absolutely dominates Yttre Skärgården, riding high over most of the lesser rock features in storm time, piling up monumental slabs of pack ice over them in winter. Intermediary is Mellan Skärgården, a zone where there is about an equal proportion of land and water, though the strength of the maritime influence is powerfully reflected in both its ecology and human activity. Of comparable areas along coastal Sweden, the Swedish novelist Selma Lagerlöf wrote that 'they didn't seem able to make up their minds whether they wanted to be land or sea'. Land takes the upper hand in Inre Skärgården; the sea is tamed and imprisoned in winding channels, shallow bays and inlets which eventually lead to the cul-de-sacs where new cultivable land is born.

Page 35 (*above*) An interior of an Åland farmhouse by K. E. Jansson, 1871; (*right*) an Ålandic fisherman by K. E. Jansson, 1869

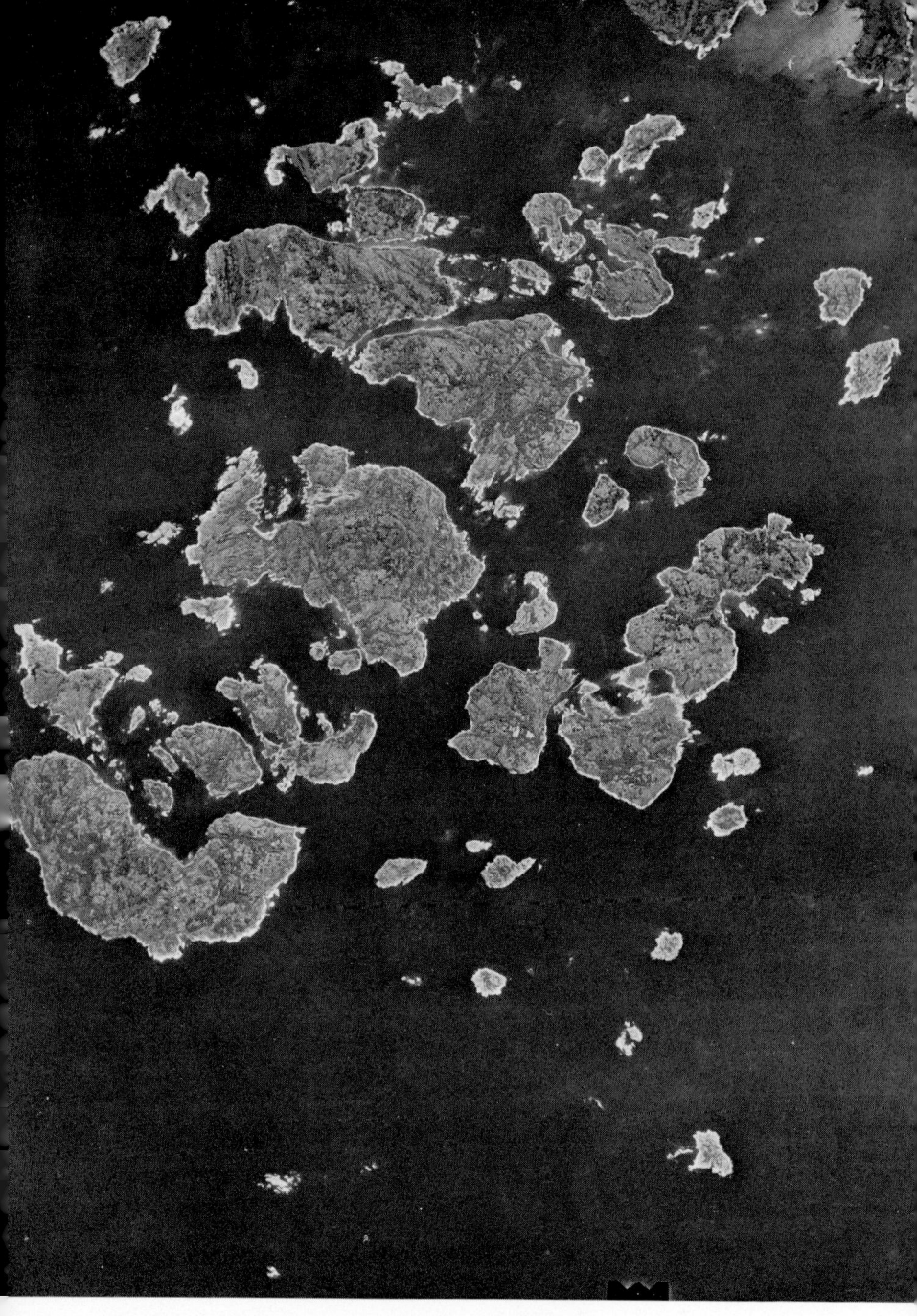

Page 36 Vertical air photograph of the island setting of Simskäla in Vårdö off
the north coast of the mainland of Åland

All of these surrounding waters are a part of the virtually enclosed Baltic Sea. Tides are consequently not perceptible around Åland and there is no critical tidewater zone. Furthermore, the salt content of its waters is low: 0·6 per cent. Not only does the salt content decline towards the heads of the larger Baltic gulfs, but it also diminishes towards the inner reaches of Åland's small *fjärdar*. Low and varying salinity presents organic life with difficult problems of adjustment. As a result, Åland's inshore waters display a meeting and mingling of both salt and fresh-water species which underlines the unusual qualities of its marine environment. Yet, although tides pulse weakly, Ålandic waters experience a strong system of maritime currents. The general movement of water is northwards through the channels of the Åboland and Åland archipelagos, and southwards along the Swedish coast. Winds and variations in air pressure also produce significant changes in water level, which can exceed a metre and cause correspondingly strong local currents in the channels of the archipelago. Variations in current, salinity and temperature conditions combine to produce favourable local environments which are critical in the distribution of fish breeding grounds.

Although water is the leading landscape feature of Åland, there is a serious deficiency of fresh water. The layer of superficial deposits that covers the impermeable bedrocks is thin and reserves of ground water are low. There are a fair number of lakes (about 160 on the main island), but they are small and shallow. Most of them also lie at a low altitude which means that chemical elements from the surrounding farmland frequently change the character of their water. Mariehamn is particularly conscious of an inadequate supply of fresh water, for most of the lakes suitable as reservoirs are located in the northern parts of the island more than 30km away. It is particularly difficult to find drinking water in the smaller islands of the outer archipelago. Wells are increasingly easy to sink, but they are expensive investments.

THE ÅLAND ISLANDS

The *rapakivi* granite, with its elaborate systems of fractures, is an element in water management which awaits fuller investigation. There are underground stream systems in it, providing the possibility of deep-seated reservoirs. Haga plain, interior Lemland and parts of Geta are probable locations; though Lumparfjärden, where the granite is overlain with younger geological formations, probably has the greatest potential. It may be conjectured that large reserves have accumulated here in the contact zone between the granite and the Cambrian and Silurian formations. Even assuming the water resources lack impurities, exploitation cannot be undertaken without considerable investment. Pollution already calls for purification of water, both in the lakes that supply the fresh-water needs of the islands and in the waters of Mariehamn's heavily used harbours.

Åland has commanded the attention of natural scientists for generations. The relationship between land and sea in the archipelagos of the Central Baltic that set vulcanologist (with his support for a theory of land upheaval) against neptunist (with his insistence on water diminution) 200 years ago, remains a matter of concern at both the theoretical and practical level. But specialisation in the natural sciences brings new insights and new techniques to bear upon the familiar issues. At the micro-level, it is the geochemist with his powerful electronic equipment who re-assesses the nature of the rocks; at the macro-level, it is the geophysicist. Simultaneously, the geochronologist gathers together information from a variety of cognate disciplines in order to build up a more refined picture of the evolution of the archipelago. The genesis of Åland has implications for an understanding of the Inner Baltic which have yet to be fully realised.

3   THE WAYS OF THE WEATHER

THE climate of the Åland archipelago is conditioned by its location in high latitudes and by its setting in an area where westerly cyclonic air streams encounter continental controls. High latitude brings with it a relatively pronounced seasonal rhythm of daylight and darkness. The continental high pressure tends to prevail in winter, especially in February and March, and in summer, especially in June and July; but cyclonic systems can intrude upon it throughout the year. An element of inconstancy therefore characterises Åland's weather. Inconstancy is repeated at the local level as a result of the intermixture of land and water, the diurnal shifts of breezes, the alternation of exposure and shelter in landscape and seascape. In common with that of other areas, the climate of Åland has also displayed long period inconstancy. In contrast to other areas, the longer term fluctuations have tended to have an exaggerated consequence for Åland, both because of its high latitude setting and because of its recent geological history.

LONGER-TERM CLIMATIC CHANGES

The post-glacial history of the Baltic area indicates that the climate has experienced pronounced variations since the frontier of the ice sheet retreated from south Finland about 10,000 years ago. The sequence of developments, based principally upon the analysis of pollen grains, is usually divided into four periods. The first is called the Boreal period (c 6550–5000 BC). It was characterised by a relatively warm and continental type of climate during which hazel, pine and birch advanced over northern Europe. The second is named the Atlantic period (c 5000–2500 BC). It coincided partly with the conversion of the Baltic Sea into the Ancylus Lake, and was marked by a more maritime climate during which the expansion of the oak was the principal vegetational change. The third period (c 2500–800 BC), called the sub-Boreal, is distinguished by a more continental type of climate and is accompanied by the restoration of a salt-water Baltic (or Litorina) Sea. The final or sub-Atlantic period (800 BC until the present time) has been cooler and moister. Among the responsive shifts of botanical frontiers, the expansion of the spruce has been the most striking feature.

Within these long-period climatic fluctuations, there have been shorter-term cyclical fluctuations, though knowledge about them is imprecise. It is conceivable that the remarkable gap in the settlement history of Åland between 300 BC and AD 500 is attributable to climatic deterioration. Historical times provide evidence of the kind of experience that could have depopulated Åland. During the 1860s there were several years with extremely cold winters and cool summers which resulted in serious harvest failure and famine. Such a situation could have had fatal consequences in earlier times.

The character of Åland's geological evolution since the Ice Age and the accompanying longer term climatic variations (summarised in the diagram on p 27) have been crucial for the resources and consequent human opportunities presented by the archipelago. In former times, when the economic base of the Åland Islands was narrower and the possibilities of regional exchange of products more limited, the short period climatic variations often bred hazards of disproportionate magnitude. The hazards were the greater because of the size of the units that the islands represented. To some degree, the situation remains, with economic and commercial stresses more than offsetting any amelioration of physical risks.

THE WAYS OF THE WEATHER

THE RECORD OF THE WEATHER

Parish priests, enjoined by the compilers of Sweden's *Tabellverket*, or census tables, to record any exceptional features of the weather, were the earliest to keep documentary evidence of Åland's weather. It was, however, F. W. Radloff, in his celebrated description of Åland (1795), who printed the first formal details about precipitation, wind direction and phenological conditions. Within a generation, the active secretary of the Finnish Economic Society was distributing recording instruments to parish priests and local officials with a view to compiling a more scientific record of Finland's climate. Among those who contributed to this effort was J. P. Granberg, who was provincial doctor in Finström parish from 1818 to 1842. A preliminary attempt to obtain a synoptic view of the climate of the Grand Duchy was made by the Finnish Scientific Society (*Finska Vetenskaps-Societeten*) in 1840. Åland made its contribution from 1847. More or less regular weather observations have been made since the early 1870s in Mariehamn, at Sälskär lighthouse (built 1868) and at Märket lighthouse (built 1885). All these early records are unreliable. Meteorological observations were more systematically organised during the 1880s, particularly against the background of a number of new lighthouses. From that time also date regular winter steamship connections, with the corresponding need for a record of ice conditions. A. W. Johansson, who organised a group of meteorological stations on the main island in 1911, produced the first classical study of Åland's climate (1915). Mariehamn's meteorological station, the principal in Åland and formerly in the town, is now located at the airport.

THE CYCLE OF THE SEASONS

In the Finnish context, Åland's climate is essentially maritime. This is reflected in cooler springs than those known in many

41

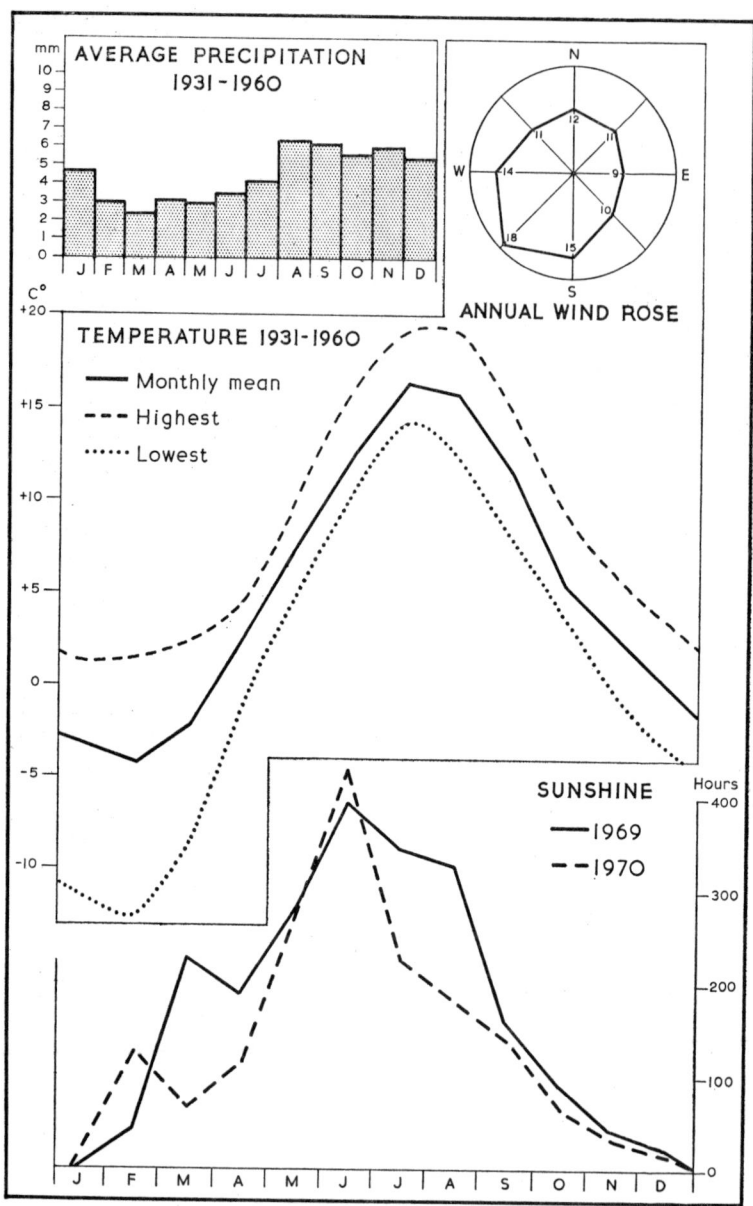

The climate of Mariehamn

parts of the country; in warmer, frost-free autumns; in higher humidity. Otherwise, the cycle of the seasons parallels that of south-western Fennoscandia. The diagram on p 44 summarises the situation.

Precipitation is relatively low (c 590mm), with the summer period (May–October) receiving the largest volume; though the number of days with precipitation (in the form of snowfall) is higher in the winter period (November–April). Spring and early summer is the driest time of the year, and April the driest month. Late July and early August have the heaviest rainfall. June has the fewest days with rain; October, the most. Annual variations of precipitation are considerable and tend to be greatest in the summer months. During winter, snowfall is fairly evenly distributed over the entire archipelago; but, during summer, the main island has a much higher rainfall than the surrounding island groups. Indeed, summer drought is a serious problem on many islands. Droughts are frequently accompanied by strong northerly winds (the north is the source of the driest air streams) which intensify evaporation from the thin soil cover and reduce ground water reserves. The intensive use of much of the cultivated land in the outer islands, especially for fruit and vegetables, has thus to contend with the risk of a shortage of fresh water. There is another difference between the situation on the main island and the surrounding archipelagos. The former experiences peak precipitation just at the time of its hay and grain harvests, both of which occur earlier than in the outlying archipelagos, where the delayed spring retards the development of crops.

The seasonal variation of temperatures is considerably reduced by maritime influences, but variations from the mean monthly temperatures can be great both in winter and summer. Humid summers and mild winters, hot summers and hard winters, reflect maritime and continental predominance respectively. Daily temperatures are closely linked to sunshine totals. In an open and low-lying landscape the impact of the sun's

43

rays is such that it frequently feels warmer than it is. Aspect is extremely important; so is local radiation. Tourists, no less than plants, are sensitive to summer's micro-climates.

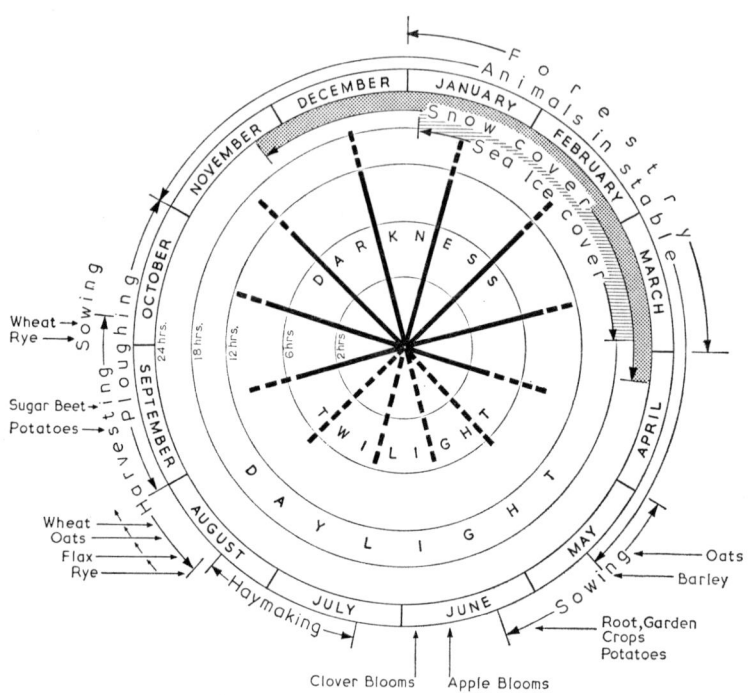

A phenological diagram for Åland mainland

In winter in general, and at the equinoxes in particular, the interplay between continental and maritime controls is expressed in rapid temperature changes. Sudden thaws alternating with hard frosts can have serious consequences for communications. the attraction of hoar frost contrasts with the distraction of ice storms. The maritime environment also gives rise to mists and fogs, especially in spring and autumn when differences between water and air temperatures are highest. April has 12 per cent and October 11 per cent of the days with fog; contrastingly, June has scarcely 4 per cent.

Winds are chiefly from the south-west, especially in summer; but north-westerlies are also common. Wind-trimmed vegetation indicates these predominant directions. July and June are calm, but the first storms already break in late August. Low pressure systems are associated with south-west and south-east air streams. High pressure systems are often accompanied by cold arctic air. In summer, the continental high pressure to the east can give hot weather with weak winds, but in winter it usually produces fierce cold, often with heavy snowstorms.

As a rule, Åland's weather is very fickle and not easily predictable. The fishing communities have traditionally taken their lives in their hands when putting to sea. Weather lore is all very well for the poet, but it is insufficient for the peasant. In Åland, it has been the fishermen rather than the farmer who has looked for signs in the sky:

> Red sky in the morning, sailor's warning:
> Red sky at night, sailor's delight.

Complementarily, he has looked at signs in the water, the level of which around his shoreline has been his primeval barometer. It is a measure of the unpredictability of Åland's weather that, despite the regularity and detail of the radio and television forecasts, the local residents remain dissatisfied.

THE WINTER CIRCUMSTANCES

The length and strength of Åland's winter can vary greatly. Winters such as that of 1972–3, without a cover of ice on the surrounding waters, are exceptional. As a rule, sea ice appears in early January and melts between the middle and end of April. In severe winters, ice can cover the whole of the Åland Sea and extend far into the southern Baltic. Wind and wave action greatly affects the local character of the sea ice. Pancake ice is compacted into drift ice, drift ice is piled up into pack ice. Ramparts of pack ice build up around the skerries according to wind direction and the fetch of the waves. In hard and turbulent winters, pack ice may extend for kilometres out from the coasts. Easterly winds can build up especially impenetrable barriers on the Swedish side of the Åland Sea.

In former times, when sleigh, ski and *sparkstötting* (a chair on runners which found its way into Åland from Sweden in the mid-nineteenth century) were the traditional means of winter communication, the establishment of firm sea ice was critical. The skate, only effective on a smooth surface, was less frequently employed. The snow scooter, employing an old principle but a new form of energy, is no less dependent upon the establishment of a satisfactory surface than its antecedents. Tractor and automobile are even more so. The establishment and persistence of a satisfactory surface is dependent upon a variety of local circumstances. Marine currents between the islands, however modest their speed, retard ice formation and make for treacherous zones of weakness in the early stages of ice formation. The nature of snow fall in relation to temperature and turbulence promotes or retards the formation of sea ice. Given quiet conditions, it can reduce the surface temperature of the water and assist the formation of a film of ice. Equally, soft snow can wreck the surface of established ice by forming a layer of slush on top of it. In theory, the hovercraft should provide a useful form of transport to cope with such conditions. The larger ferries can contend with most forms of sea ice, though, if need be, icebreakers are available to maintain open channels. Not infrequently, ferry channels cut across old-established winter sleighing routes.

Winter icing (*isläggning*, to use the local phrase) imposes immediate restraints on daily life. In earlier times, it was accompanied by a retreat to indoor occupations and handicrafts, supplemented by a little forestry, occasional ice-hole fishing and sealing, if weather permitted. Today, fishermen migrate with their larger trawlers to the open waters of the central or southern Baltic, use such harbours as Slite in Gotland as winter bases, and may be absent from home for months on end.

A MATTER OF RELATIVITY

Åland's climate has the same ingredients as that of the rest of Finland; it is the proportions in which they are mixed that are different. For Åland, as for Finland, long, usually warm summer days have their antithesis in short, invariably cold winter days. It is in the duration of summer that Åland scores. A record of the thermal seasons (1931–60) gives to Åland an average of 117 days of summer; 106 of winter; 59 of spring and 83 of autumn. In this respect, the archipelago experiences the most favourable climatic conditions of any part of Finland and more favourable conditions than most parts of Sweden.

Again, although the northerly element in its setting must not be underestimated, it must not be exaggerated. The Åland archipelago lies in the same latitudes as the Orkneys. Accordingly, its daylight–darkness rhythms are the same. If Åland's winters have acquired a legendary severity, it is low temperatures that lend them their character, and the brighter, drier weather that accompanies them would be regarded by some as preferable to the frequent gales that lash their Atlantic counterparts. Furthermore, the very equableness of the temperature of the Orkneys or Shetlands robs them of the radiance that is the usual quality of an Åland summer.

4   GARDEN OF THE NORTHERN HESPERIDES

A PERMISSIVE ENVIRONMENT

ÅLAND has an unusually rich flora. It claims nearly 700 of the 1,000 species that occur in Finland. The number of different plants is only about fifty less than that found in the island of Gotland, which is more than double the size of Åland, has a more amenable bedrock and lies farther south. The mainland Finnish provinces of Nyland and Egentliga Finland have lower totals despite their much greater extent.

Several facts explain this situation. Firstly, there are the characteristics of the *skärgård* landscape; fracturing has produced a large number of separate units of land, each of which offers special circumstances for plant colonisation. Secondly, there is the absolute length of the coast which favours invasion by plants and animals. Thirdly, secular land uplift (c 55cm per century) continuously exposes new tracts for colonisation in front of the existing coastal zone and thereby offers opportunities for continuous biological innovation. This dynamic element in the environment is exceptional. But diversity in the environment continues even back from the shoreline, with local topography and local climates producing a landscape of remarkable contrasts. In it, changes in the content of soil moisture and organic material consequent upon land upheaval, make for a greater variety of development in natural processes than is encountered in most places. All these terrestrial circumstances are inseparable from the combination of maritime and continental qualities of Åland's climate. A fifth point in the explanation of Åland's flora is that the northern coniferous forest (*barrskog*, as it is called) has never played such a dominant role as on the mainland to the west and east of the archipelago. The more southerly plant species that invaded Åland, partly over Sweden and partly by way of Baltic routes, have never had to compete to the same degree with the sturdier vegetational constituents they would have encountered, for example, in Nyland.

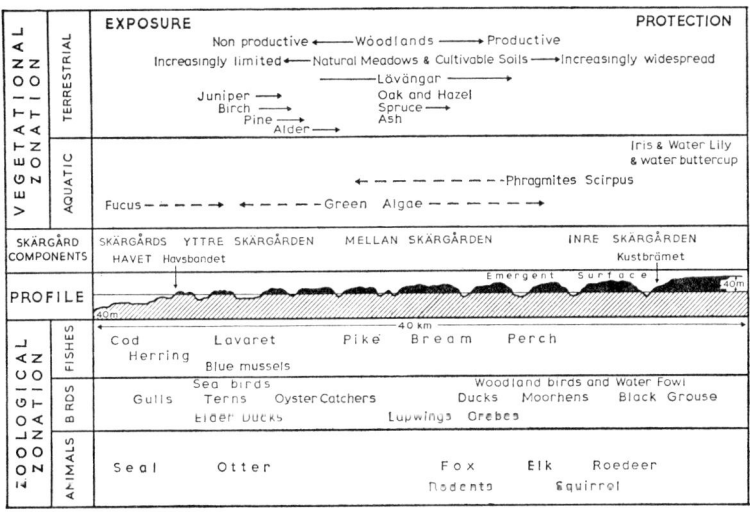

An ecological traverse through Åland mainland

The range of Åland's vegetation is broad. As a result of its location and geographical circumstances, it accommodates some of the northernmost occurrences of a number of southern Scandinavian plants, and some of the most southerly outliers of a number of northern Scandinavian species. Nearly a fifth of Åland's flora, or about 126 species, consists of plants that have more southerly origins. In Åland, they mingle with pre-

49

dominantly high latitude species. The extreme in antithesis is between the winter-shy yew and the sub-Arctic species that occupy the coastal zone of the outer skerries. On the cold, exposed rocks of the maritime fringe, the birch and the juniper assume forms comparable to those displayed in parts of Finnish Lapland, though their plant community also includes the alder (*Alnus glutinosa*) and mountain ash (*Sorbus aucuparia*). Embraced in the 'birch zone' are the whole of Brändö parish and most of Kökar, though Kökar formerly had some softwood stands.

Åland's vegetation also juxtaposes moisture-loving and drought-resistant species. The boglands and the deciduous woodlands, with their luxuriant undergrowth, are poles apart from the communities associated with the meagre and dry soils of the rock outcrops. Here, plants are powerfully modified to cope with conditions of drought. Communities of xerophytes or near xerophytes result. They range from the tufted ling and cowberry to a variety of fleshy-leaved stone-crops (*Sedum acre, Sedum album, Sedum telephium*). A different type of xerophytic vegetation occurs on the thin soils of the hillocks and hill slopes that surround the meadows. Here, drought-resistant grasses (*Festuca* and *Bromus*) are associated with the rock rose (*Helianthemum nummularia*), wild spinach (*Laserpitium latifolium*) and crane's bill (*Geranium sanguineum*).

In transverse section, from seashore to interior rocky highland, the generalised distribution would show in succession: 1 a birch zone; 2 a pine zone; 3 deciduous woodland and meadowland in competition with spruce; 4 spruce transitional to pine; 5 pine. But, since generalisations exist to be broken, in any given zone exceptions might locally exceed the rule.

For statistical purposes, Åland's vegetation falls into three broad categories. First, there are the woodlands, which cover about half the surface area and are absolutely dominated by softwoods. Secondly, there is the cultivated area, accounting for about 10 per cent. In its original state, much of the cleared area bore deciduous woods. Residual stands of the original timber remain around the cultivated area. The remaining 30 per cent of the surface consists of what the census defines as *impedimenter*—rock outcrops of one kind or another, together with boulder and cobble fields.

LIFE ON THE SEASHORE

In Åland, life began—and continues to begin—on the seashore. The shoreline has two basic forms: a sedimentary form and a rocky form. Sedimentary shorelines are most extensive around the inner islands; hard rock shorelines are absolutely dominant in the outer skerries.

Sedimentary shorelines have their fullest manifestation around the heads of inlets. In the shallow, brackish waters that are inhabited by perch, pike and bream, the sea bed supports a tangled growth of milfoil, pond weeds, water buttercups and even water lilies. These merge with the dense fringe of reeds, rushes and scattered yellow irises. *Arundo phragmites*, often 1·5m or more tall, stands out with its feathery brown plumes as the most common, though bulrushes are also found. Waterfowl nest in their protection; dragonflies dart above them. Landwards, they yield to the saltings, where arrow grass (*Triglochin maritimum*) provides good grazing for cattle. The seashore pastures also support dense thickets of seabuckthorn (*Hippophaës rhamnoides*). *Hippophaës*, its branches thick with orange-coloured berries, made a great impression on early naturalists—*in maritimis Alandiae copiosissima*, wrote Christopher Tärnström. *Sesleria coerulea*, a decorative grass, is an indicator of relatively high lime content in the soil. Angelica, valerian, grass of Parnassus and the wild aster are joined by the distinctive *Primula farinosa*.

Hard rock shorelines are skirted by a thick growth of toffee-coloured *Fucus vesiculosis*, which may extend to depths of 8m. Although perch and pike are also found here, cod, flat-fish and, above all, Baltic herring take precedence. Along the flanks of the bare rock and boulders, just above the limit of high water and winter ice, *Verrucaria maura*—a black lichen—paints a dark band. It is on these hard landfalls that plants first colonised Åland—water, wind and winged creatures each bearing their contributions. The process continues today, with powerful variations on the original themes played by human agencies.

THE ROCK GARDENS

Associated with the hard rock shorelines is one of Åland's most fascinating features. If the *lövängar*—the deciduous woodland glades—are Åland's equivalent to the gardens of the Hesperides, the granite exposures of the outer *skärgård* are nature's ready-made rock gardens. In them, a few dozen square metres can display textbook examples of the facts governing plant distribution, adaptation, succession and colonisation. Across their surfaces—fractured, weathered, polished by ice, pock-marked by solution—critical thresholds of plant occurrence are drawn pencil-sharp. In the fullest sense of the word, these rocky skerries are a botanist's paradise, with fertility and sterility infinite in their juxtapositions.

At the humblest vegetational level, fertility becomes apparent in seeming sterility, for the granite itself supports many of the 1,500 different lichens that are indigenous to Åland. Lichen is a botanical miracle, the qualities of which can only be fully realised with the aid of a magnifying glass. In colour, the lichens range from grey, through sage green, olive, viridian, pale mustard, red-brown to charcoal. Some, such as *Rhizocarpon obscuritum*, simply powder the rock surface with their misty growth. Others, such as the ochrous *Rhizocarpon geographicum*, engrave mapmakers' nightmares on the tables of stone. Some, such as *Parmelia tilliacea*, emboss the rock flanks with velvet patterns; some, like *Parmelia fuliginosa*, blemish the rock face with their dark excoriations. The foliose lichens may sketch rosettes only a few centimetres across or inscribe roundels a metre or more in diameter. By the very act of living on the rock,

Page 53 Sellskär in the outer archipelago. In the background are the ice-sculptured rocks and the gale-swept scanty vegetation

Page 54 (above) The inner archipelago, with typical architecture in the foreground and showing a bridge and causeway connecting the islands; (below) Käringsund in Eckerö parish, showing the traditional boatsheds and a modern trawler in the foreground they make their own infinitesimal contribution to its disintegration. Aesthetically, lichens are the perfect foil to the pink *rapakivi* granite, in combination with which their pastel shades have inspired a good many designers.

Landwards, the juniper, too, is a source of inspiration. In association with the lithe birch, it accepts to the full the challenge of exposure and a rocky foothold. It adopts a completely different form from the erect and tapering outline that it displays inland. Here, it extends over the rock surface in trim, green carpets. It branches out in all directions until it exhausts itself, then bequeaths a tangle of tough, grey roots and branches to be cast around the beaches as driftwood fantasies. As for the pines, no potted trees ever responded more pliantly to the demands of a Japanese gardener than they to their rocky bowls. To see a scurry of cones driven across the lichened rock to the false security of fissured resting places is to anticipate a new generation of pines tested to the limits of endurance. In the rock-gardens, a mature pine may be only a metre or so high, the contortions of its branches complementing the exposed root system which, in its frantic search for moisture and nourishment, casts a network over the surface of the rock like veins on the back of a countryman's hands.

The rock garden has a different expression on the sea-lashed reefs where tree and shrub give up the unequal struggle. Here, the mood derives in part from the bird colonies that use the reefs as breeding grounds. The soil that develops in the interstices between the boulders and in the cracks between the disintegrating rocks has a high content of nitrate as well as lime. This derives from bird droppings and from the disintegrating shells of the blue mussel that is much beloved of the eider duck. Lyme grass (*Elymus arenarius*) and hair grass (*Deschampsia bottnica*) find a ready foothold. Wild currants and wild strawberries soon establish themselves in the sea-wrack that rots between the stones. The brightness of the sun and the light reflected from the water and rock give an unusual brilliance to

D

the flora—from the mustard-coloured splashes of the lichen, *Xanthorria*, through the yellows of the bedstraw and the Compositae to the lollipop pink of the wild rose, the purple of the loosestrife (*Lythrum salicaria*) and the blue of campanulas.

THE FLORISTIC CLIMAX

The central European deciduous woodlands have their northernmost outpost in Åland. Since their plant communities were easily recognised as a guide to good soils, they made an impact on the early inhabitants. They were partly cleared for cultivation, partly left as *lövängar*. Because of Åland's topography, they are not such extensive features as in the Swedish islands of Gotland and Öland. They have been most frequently restricted to the heads of inlets, to small valleys between the rocky ridges and to the margins of land cleared for cultivation from the original leafwoods.

The *lövängar* are in the fullest sense of the word a part of the cultural landscape. Their persistence depends on the careful maintenance of a special relationship between trees, bushes and natural meadow. Ash, oak, elm, lime, maple, hazel and rowan are fashioned into an open park-like tract through trimming and cutting in spring and through leaf gathering, especially for sheep, in early August. A midsummer hay crop is commonly cut from the grass which is subsequently grazed. The result has been a pollarded landscape, though rather more open than the pollarded woodlands of the English Weald. In contrast to the English scene, however, the *lövängar* are especially vulnerable to invasion by the spruce. Around the clumps of trees and between the hazel stumps, there is a rich assemblage of grasses and flowering plants. In the spring, viburnum, bird cherry, wild plum and hawthorn bloom above carpets of blue and white anemones, lilies of the valley, wild garlic, violets and primroses. Spiraeas and Solomon's seal stand beside orchids, eleven species of which are either absent or are only

56

rarely encountered on the Finnish mainland. The wild strawberry proliferates around their margins.

Conservation alone is insufficient to protect the *lövängar*, since they are the product of a traditional form of land use. Once they suffer a decline into ordinary pasture, the number of plant species dwindles. Once the balance between grazing and cutting is destroyed, the spruce invades. Ramsholm, near Mariehamn, was formerly a show piece. Here the quality of the flora has been lost through proximity to the built-up area. True *lövängar* persist in Finström, west of Bamböle; in Geta, around Bolstaholm; in Eckerö, north of Storby; in Hammarland, around Äppelö. More than 300 different plants are found in the *lövängar*: 45 of them trees and bushes; 47 of them grasses; the rest flowering species. Probably the finest example is Idö in Kökar parish—an island less than 1,500m in length on which 200 plant species occur. Granholm in Lemland contains an equally remarkable concentration on an island 700m long and only 400m at its greatest breadth. It includes the yew (*Taxus baccata*) which is only found in about two other places in Åland. The Botany Bays of such islands are unspoiled by historical undertones.

WOODLANDS AND BOGLANDS

Two-thirds of Åland's wooded area consists of productive timberlands, half of which are pine stands. The pine is the hardiest of Åland's trees, and dominates all of the sterile tracts. On the high rocky plateau-like surfaces of northern Åland, it grows to the exclusion of almost everything else. In striking contrast to the *lövängar*, the pine woods only muster about sixty other species in their plant community. The spruce is the dominant conifer on the flatter lands and advances up the hill slopes where and when soil moisture conditions permit. As a result of this and of their sensitivity to wind, spruce woods are only fully developed on the larger islands. They comprise about 30 per cent of the productive woodlands. The birch accounts for

9 per cent; the aspen, for 2 per cent. The components of the deciduous woodlands claim so modest a share as to be almost negligible.

Yet, it is the deciduous trees that give Åland's landscape its distinction. The most common is the ash (*Fraxinus excelsior*); the frequency of its occurrence, both in its natural state and as a planted tree, is more generous than anywhere on the Finnish mainland. Its bouquets of light green leaves with their bunches of winged seeds have an exotic appearance by Finnish standards. *Sorbus fennica*, the Ålandic rowan—which in both leaf form and berry is a sturdier manifestation of the mountain ash—is a distinctive native species. The maple (*Acer platanoides*) is the most colourful component. The oak (*Quercus robur*) formerly played a critical local role for shipbuilding. The elm (*Ulmus glabra*), crab apple (*Pyrus malus*) and hawthorn (*Crataegus*) are also species common to Åland, but much more rarely encountered on the mainland.

Most of Åland's timber stands were considerably neglected until after World War II. With the steady rise in the price of timber, growing attention has been paid to the woodland. As a consequence, birchwood stands are being reduced and softwoods improved and extended. Firstly, softwoods regenerate more speedily than hardwoods. Secondly, they are sensitive to destruction through fire—and forest fires are caused more frequently through lightning than through human carelessness. Thirdly, while early summer is the floristic climax of the deciduous woodlands, late summer and early autumn are the time of greatest appeal in the coniferous woodlands. It is the season when the berry-bearing ground flora yields its harvest and the mycologist enters his season of ecstasy. The blueberry, moist in its carpet of mosses, accompanies the spruce; the lingon, often set in grey-green reindeer moss (*Cladonia*) is the ground flora of the pine woods. Finally, with more than 2,000 different kinds of mushrooms and fungi, Åland's coniferous woodlands are typical of the northern *barrskog*.

GARDEN OF THE NORTHERN HESPERIDES

The maritime climate, coupled with the broken terrain, gives rise to a fair sprinkling of lakes and swamps; as a rule, both are small. On mainland Åland, there are 160 lakes, but only three of them—west and east Kyrksunden and Långsjön—are sizeable. Lakes occur at different altitudes. Because of land uplift, few parts of Finland have lakes of so many different biological types in so small a compass as Åland. There is also a contrast between the richly vegetated lakes of the southern plains of mainland Åland and the swampy lakes of north Åland. Thanks to the lime content in the soil, the margins of the lowland lakes (and bogs) usually have a more varied flora than those of the lakes and bogs on the higher land.

Although boglands are widely scattered, extensive natural peatlands are restricted to the so-called Stormossen in Lemland. This was formerly a labyrinth of swampy waterways and a favourite haunt of elk. It has, however, been largely drained in order to encourage colonisation by timber. The peatlands are a happy hunting ground for bryologists—Åland having bred its own specialists in the study of mosses over a century ago. The peatlands support a generous growth of *Myrica gale* and bog cotton. Cranberries are common; cloudberries less so.

THE FAUNA

Although there are well over 5,000 different kinds of living creatures in Åland, only a limited number make a visible impact by comparison with the wide-ranging flora. Among mammals, the elk is still the most impressive and maintains its numbers. The roe deer (introduced 1945–7) is increasing. Both are hunted under permit in the autumn. Among predators, the red fox, marten, ermine and wild mink are quite widespread. The wolf and lynx have been extinct for a century. The otter and hare contrive in their particular ways to find food throughout the winter. The hedgehog adopts a torpid attitude to it; so, too, does the squirrel. And, since Eden cannot exist without its serpents, the viper successfully eludes the winter cold in order to bask on the hot summer rocks.

Seals still appear in the skerries, but the considerable numbers that once attracted winter hunters and yielded such a legacy of stories and legends have been largely destroyed. The most common seal is *Phoca hispida*; the grey seal (*Halichaerus grypus*) only appears rarely. While the disappearance of the seal and the otter is largely attributable to man, the absence of lowlier marine life is mostly a reflection of natural restraints. Many creatures familiar in west European coastal waters die out around Åland: sea anemone and sea cucumber, crab and whelk. Others, such as the heart mussel (*Cardium edule*) and water snails, are reduced in size.

Bird life has a contrasting vitality. Rather more than 100 species are found in Åland. To each habitat belongs a particular community of birds; the number per square kilometre in the needlewoods is only two-fifths of that in the leaf woods. The coniferous woods harbour the game birds—above all, the capercaillie. Just occasionally, the sea eagle sails above the rocky eminences of north Åland, but it is estimated that fewer than a dozen pairs remain in the archipelago. Falcon and sparrowhawk are also rare. To the leaf woods belong a great variety, if not a great number of birds, mostly migratory—finches, tits, flycatchers, cuckoos. Swallows and swifts move in to feast on the summer clouds of mosquitoes and midges. The cry of the corncrake is redolent of harvest time. The magpie haunts the farm yard and the town garden.

Larger birds associated with the inner islands, such as the swan, grey goose, heron and whooping crane, are also migratory. Most sea birds retreat to the open water in the face of winter's advancing ice edge. They return, with open water to the bird skerries (*fågelskär*) for the nesting season. The eggs of seagulls, grey-backed gulls and herring gulls hatch at the end of May or early June; those of the fishing terns and silver terns, a fortnight later; the tufted duck and other ducks, between midsummer and mid-July; some, even later. Eider and other ducks keep the sea birds company, their chicks appearing in early June. The oystercatcher and sandpiper are also favourite Åland birds. The habits of sea birds in Åland have been the subject of detailed study since before World War I. In recent years, they have been ringed by the tens of thousand. All are subject to varying degrees of protection.

GRANITE AND WATER

'It is *ensembles* that count,' wrote a French naturalist a century ago. In this case, it is an *ensemble* at two levels. First, there is the *ensemble* of Åland as a whole, distinct among Baltic archipelagos and therefore unique. Secondly, there is the totality of natural elements out of which is created the individuality of each constituent island. To walk across an island is to receive a number of swiftly changing impressions. Simplicity yields to complexity, fertility to sterility, affluence to poverty. The basic quality of the natural scene derives from the close juxtaposition of opposites. At its most simple, it is the juxtaposition of granite and water. To employ a classical metaphor, complexity enters as soon as Flora intercedes with Pluto and Neptune. Where they yield, the botanical result is, in the words of Håkan Kulves, 'sub-tropical fertility'; where they deny, 'near lunar sterility'. But there are other dimensions involved in the traverse of any sizeable Ålandic island. First, such an island will contain a microcosm of the landscapes of Fennoscandia—from the rock gardens of the Skagerrak to the fells of Lapland by way of deciduous woodlands and coniferous forests, birch groves and lichen pastures, diminutive counterparts of the clay plains of Uppland and Finland proper, token lakescapes, incipient boglands, boulder tracts and sand wastes. Secondly, any traverse involves a temporal experience. Since the archipelago has been and is being born of the sea, to cross an island is to pass through a part of the physical evolution experienced by the whole archipelago in former millennia. Thirdly, something of a spiritual experience can result from the totality of these impressions. It is often as though unreality marched close beside reality. In another context, Virginia Woolf compared the moments when reality and unreality come together as 'the unlikely marriage' of granite and the rainbow. In Åland, where summer rainbows frequently arc down to the granite, marriages of this kind are more common than in most places.

5 THE DEVELOPMENT OF SOCIETY AND ECONOMY

T HE Åland archipelago has about it the feel of long occupation—long, that is to say, by Scandinavian standards. Centuries of occupation have left their particular marks on the landscape—some much eroded by natural forces, some near obliterated by technical change, some remarkably persistent because of the generous legacy of knowledge about the land and resources that has been transmitted through successive generations of Ålanders. For all the overlay of modern living, past ways of life are more than folk memories. Moreover, they have persisted long enough for them to be respected and protected. Ålanders are aware that in them is rooted a part of their distinguishing heritage. In addition, they realise that the capital and labour patiently invested in their islands by earlier generations have created a landscape to be enjoyed in a new leisure age and which is therefore worthy of protection for its own sake.

THE PREHISTORIC SETTLEMENT

The prehistoric settlement of the Åland Islands is a reflection of their changing shape, of their changing climate and of a location midway between the Scandinavian and the Baltic cultural areas. The islands have been occupied continuously for about 6,000 years. The present contour level of 55m approximates to the outline of the Åland archipelago at the beginning of Stone Age settlement. Analysis of pollen grains from residual peat

63

bogs in the higher parts of Åland suggests that Neolithic settlers experienced a climate similar to that of the present. There is little material evidence of their hunting and fishing culture; but settlement sites have yielded sufficient fragments of ceramic ware for the Stone Age (c 3000–1800 BC) to be defined in terms of the designs and forms of its pottery. The best-known Stone Age site is at Jettböle in Jomala parish. From the same site, though later in age, have been discovered a number of clay figurines. Although no indigenous flint stones were available for the fashioning of the arrowheads and axe blades of Stone Age hunters, a flint-like prophyry was widely employed to supplement imports. Onega green slate and red Scandinavian slate were also imported. These raw materials were basic to the tools and weapons of the so-called Boat Axe Culture (c 2000 BC) and examples are glass-cased in Mariehamn's museum.

The first marks on the land belong to the earlier Bronze Age and consist of grave mounds which resemble those of the west Scandinavian culture area. Among the ones at Grytverksnäset in Sund paris is a setting of stones in the shape of a ship. There are also well-preserved Bronze Age dwelling sites— among them, Otterböte in Kökar parish, with its nine clearly identifiable hut floors, is the most impressive. Thousands of pottery fragments, believed to be the remains of clay crocks in which seal oil was transported, have been recovered from the site. Articles of bronze, very limited in occurrence, recall the need for import of metals. After about 500 BC there is a general decline in archaeological remains which has given rise to much speculation. There may have been a decline in settlement consequent upon a worsening climate or a diminution in artefacts attributable to changing cultural habits.

Although the Finnish Iron Age is generally reckoned to have lasted 1,000 years and therefore overlaps the beginnings of recorded history in western Europe, it was not until the latter part of the so-called period of migrations (AD 550–800) that it left a significant imprint on the Ålandic scene. In fact, the Iron Age cemeteries of Åland are one of the most distinctive features of its human landscape. Åland has 440 known burial fields from about AD 500–1000. Some, layered successively with cremated remains and stones, cover hundreds of square metres. There are about 10,000 identified grave mounds, some 2,400 in Saltvik alone. In addition, there are at least thirty boat burial sites closely resembling those at Vendel in Swedish Uppland. House sites are less readily apparent, but about 100 from the latter half of the Iron Age have been identified. As on mainland Finland, there are a number of fortified rock outcrops, called *borg*, as in Borgboda (Saltvik parish) and Borgberget (Hammarland parish). Stone labyrinths, which rejoice in the name of *jungfrudansar*, are found in Lemland and Kökar. The Iron Age sites of Åland have yielded considerable treasure trove. The products of itinerant metal workers and weapon smiths vary from finely tooled ornaments and brooches to substantial weapons, such as the find at Syllöda in Saltvik from c AD 600. Evidence for a developing trading community lies in a scatter of gold ornaments of Iron Age provenance (for example, from the Gölby grave in Jomala) and in the diversity of coins minted in lands as far apart as Gaul and the Near East.

To the realities of Dark Age life, posterity has added a touch of romance. At least one school of thought sees in Åland the setting for some of the myths incorporated in *Kalevala*, the best-known part of Finland's folk lore. There are philological grounds for speculating that Lemminkäinen, the Don Juan of Finnish mythology, might have had his roots in Lemland and Lemböle. Botanically speaking, the legendary island (Saari) where he conducted his flirtations was more likely to belong to the Åland archipelago than to any other part of Finland.

Meanwhile, Åland was absorbed into the Viking orbit and the Swedish rather than the Baltic culture area. The grave mounds die out, but treasure trove points to a common way of life. Åland has yielded distinctively Scandinavian brooches and arm rings, gaming pieces and ornamental combs. Finds of coins in Geta and, above all, in Saltvik, suggest increasingly active exchange in the ninth and tenth centuries. Two silver coins discovered in a bottle at Bertby in Saltvik are Arabic and suggest wider trading or raiding in the east.

Several important developments characterised later Viking times. First, there was a slow crystallisation of regular shipping routes. Long before the earliest remaining documents of sailing instructions through the Baltic were written down, the principal Åland shipping channels were faithfully followed. Generations of traders had followed them, bartering their goods or acquiring them for the miscellaneous coinage of half the old world. By late Viking times, they came in vessels called *kugge* or *kogge*, a word which has given rise to a sprinkling of place names—Kuggsund, Kuggdrag, Kuggböle. *Navigatio ex Dania per mare Balticum ad Estoniam*, a parchment from about 1250 in Stockholm's Royal Library, contains the record of the accumulated experience. It also appears to have been compiled by a Danish bishop, which reflects the concern of the Church for the area.

A second development was the penetration of Christian influences. The first missionary journeys in the north are presumed to have been undertaken by Ansgar of Bremen and are dated 856. The end point of his journey is usually recognised as Birka, a major concentration of settlement from the Viking age on an island in Lake Mälaren in south-central Sweden. There is little doubt that conditions in Åland in the tenth century closely resembled those of the Mälar area—indeed, if anything, its fishing and hunting provided richer bases for providing a livelihood. Åland appears to have received missionary impulses at least as early as the Mälar area, and probably earlier than most of the Swedish province of Uppland. In contrast to the situation on the Swedish mainland, Åland is curiously lacking in rune stones. Some would argue that their absence in Åland is a reflection of its earlier christianisation. Exactly when the missionaries first arrived is debatable. In

Sund churchyard, a cross bearing a runic inscription is interpreted as being a memorial to a missionary, Wenni, who brought the gospel to the islands. One insistent Ålandic school of thought has mustered evidence to give a very creditable case to the argument that Birka itself was located in Åland. In this twilight age between heathendom and christendom, the islands began to escape from anonymity and place names to acquire permanence. First, there are those of beacon hills, such as Kasberg and Vårdberget, the fires of which continued into the Christian era to give warning of the approach of sea robbers from Novgorod and Estonia. Secondly, there are names related to heathen places of worship: Smör, as in Smörholm, Smörklint, Smörnabbe, is associated with fertility rites. Trollholm, Torsäng (Thor's meadow) and Dansarberget are cult names that speak for themselves. Christian nomenclature provides a third complementary group, as illustrated by the 'cross' names of Korsnäs, Korsbacka, Korsudda. Names deriving from the world of nature are probably equally old. Examples are provided by the bird islands: Gåsö (goose island), Kråkskär (crow skerry), Måsskär (gull island); the plant islands: Rönnskär (rowan island), Enskär (juniper skerry), Lökö (wild onion island); and the animal islands: Sälskär (seal skerry), Ryssö (horse island), Elgskär (elk skerry), Björnholma (bear island). Settlement appears to have intensified with the missionary thrust, so that by the twelfth century to the existing *torp*, or homestead, names were added those of new hamlets and farms. One of the commonest elements associated with the colonisation was the suffix *böle*, a dwelling place. Some forty settlement names contain this element. Dynasties of settlements bearing the suffix *boda* were established, often on the site of the summer shielings—Skogboda, Overboda, Hästboda.

THE ORGANISATION OF ÅLAND

The first incipient organisation of Åland became apparent a

its people emerged from the Viking age. Åland, like Gotland, was originally divided into three parts or *tredingar*; central to them were Finström, Saltvik and Jomala. To each was appointed a *lagman* whose business it was to conduct the assembly, or *ting*. Tingsbacka is a place name recalling this feature and a monument has been erected beside Saltvik church to commemorate what is probably Åland's oldest assembly ground.

The division of Åland was accompanied by the introduction of new ideas—practical as well as spiritual—by the early churchmen. The first churchmen established small chapels along the leads to and through the islands, such as Signildskär on the outermost skerries in the west, Lemböte (the church ruins of which remain today), and Källskatan in Kökar parish. To Kökar also came a little colony of Franciscan monks, with their chapel and refuge for travellers at Hamnö, beside the site now occupied by the parish church. The stone well, from which they obtained their water, may still be seen; the so-called monks' fields may still be identified, and the Monk's Mill in Karlby, where their grain was ground, is still remembered. The grey friars, with their concern for the practical and their close links with their parent monastery in Stockholm, no doubt introduced new crops and stock for the island's farmers. Cattle were to play an especially important role around the edges of the economy. The friars also introduced new fishing techniques.

The importance of the archipelago as a stepping stone on the route to semi-heathen Finland, as well as the need to protect it from the robbers of the East Baltic, led to its fortification. Fortified churches, wooden stave structures (the meagre relics of which have been found at Finström and Saltvik) preceded the solid buildings of metre-long granite blocks and boulders—heavily vaulted, sturdily towered, round-arched, with dedications to the new northern saints Olaf and Brigitta as well as the old—that began to rise in the thirteenth century. These are sometimes called 'speckled-hen' churches, because of the reddish brown and grey rock colours between the plaster.

DEVELOPMENT OF SOCIETY AND ECONOMY

The churches in turn anticipated Åland's fortress of Kastelholm, the central parts of which date from the latter half of the fourteenth century. To its keep and tower, built to withstand the assaults of both foreign enemies and opposition elements in turbulent medieval Sweden, were added brick and stone extensions to accommodate the growing number of administrators, soldiery and servants. As befitted an island fortress, Kastelholm acquired its own shipyard in the sixteenth century and employed fifty shipwrights. The castle was to know princely processions, perambulations and imprisonments. Gustavus Vasa was to stay here as a boy. Eric XIV, one time suitor of Elizabeth I of England, was to be imprisoned here in 1570—his attachment to Karin Månsdotter providing the inspiration for romantic painters of three centuries later. Erik Dahlberg, Sweden's baroque cartographer, deemed it worthy of inclusion in his panoramic *Suecia antiqua et hodierna* (1665–1700), a volume which also presented the first copper-plate impression of Åland's coat-of-arms—a gilded hart wearing a ringed collar in a blue field. The Swedish monarchy used Kastelholm regularly as a residence during royal elk shoots—which inspired an opera, *Carl XII's Hunt*, with music by F. Pacius and words by Z. Topelius, in 1852. It was largely from Kastelholm that the law was to be administered, that order was to be maintained, that chroniclers were to put about their tales and that Åland's sorry bout of witch hunting (no fewer than eighteen cases in the century following 1544) was to be initiated. The royal farms (*kungsgårdar*) of Kastelholm, Greslby in Finström and Haga in Sund, and the entailed estates (*frälsegårdar*)—the coats-of-arms of whose owners still embellish church walls—looked to it as the symbol of the crown. In Kastelholm, new authority was to be invested following the Reformation.

Meanwhile, churches were adorned with the art of the day. Finström, Sund and Kumlinge are regarded as displaying the best of their kind in Scandinavian church art. Stone carvings, such as the giant's head in Finström and the lion's head in

Jomala, are believed to be the work of twelfth-century crafts-men. There are fourteenth-century church furnishings, such as the Gotland Madonna in Lemland; wood carvings of the Cologne school, such as the apostles in Sund; crucifixes and altar pieces of Lübeck craftsmen, as in Finström and Brändö. Only fragments of stained glass have survived Åland's turbulent history; but wall paintings have been painstakingly restored. Knights and ladies, saints and sinners, heavenly fathers and satans, stations of the cross, ships and wheels of fortune, scrolled around with floral designs, have been outlined in black and red ochre and coloured in green, grey-blue and amber. These assemblages of life-sized forms are roofed over with tarred shingles, and look down on the Gotland limestone slabs that are carved into fonts and vault coverings or are smoothed as floorings.

Colonists, traders and churchmen from across the Åland Sea rapidly stamped the archipelago with the imprint of Sweden proper, so that as life and activities became formalised they took on Swedish shapes and structures. Already by the twelfth century, legal and administrative frameworks were being introduced. Land ownership and property boundaries had to be organised. So, too, had water ownership—from lake and inlet to inshore and offshore fishing rights. The Swedish laws that crystallised in the Middle Ages had identical application to the province of Åland. Within their framework, property was exchanged, bequeathed and inherited; a number of the earliest documents appertaining to Åland deal with these matters. In the process, units of land were measured, valued and named with increasing precision.

The name of Åland itself was projected sufficiently by the fourteenth century for it to be incorporated as 'Alandia' on Marino Sanudo's world map (1320–30). The names of Ålanders began to enter west European records at the same time: in February 1340, for example, Petrus, dictus Alandensis received his baccalaureate at the University of Paris; and, in 1438–45, Magnus Petri de Alandya was a student in Leipzig and Erfurt.

Page 71
(right) Ytternäs
in Jomala in
the springtime;
(below) a country
museum at
Kastelholm

Page 72 The fortress of Kastelholm

In June 1366, Johannes Peterson of Sund parish achieved the distinction of becoming rector of Paris University. Other Ålanders established themselves as solid burghers in Stockholm, among them Peter Ålänning and Gunder Ålänning, who are remembered for the legacies of property they bequeathed to the Bishopric of Åbo.

Formal inheritance and transmission of property were features of the late medieval economy which already became manifest in Eric of Pomerania's tax book of 1413. From this document, it may also be observed that Åland's 526 *bönder*, or owner-farmers, were subject to a growing number of dues and day labours. Only those who colonised or cleared land were accorded temporary relief from the obligations. In addition to the state, the Church collected a tithe, which was successfully extended to the products of the sea. The barrelled salt herring and the split and dried cod of Åland were subject to it; so, too, was the seal cull, the tithe of which is the subject of a succession of documents, 1334-6. Some idea of the value of sealing is given in a document from 1557 which refers to twelve sealers delivering 908 skins to a dresser, Erik Berg. The oldest extant tax book dealing with Åland was bound together in a brown leather volume by bookbinder Bartolomeus of Uppsala. It is dated 1537-8 and was the first of a succession of record books covering landed property. About a dozen land registers—*Jordböcker*, as they were called—are available for Åland between 1557 and 1605. Following the Reformation and the reorganisation of taxation under Gustavus Vasa, dues were imposed upon land with progressive refinement according to its quality and use, upon fixed property and upon production. The registers identify taxable butter, corn, malt, meal, hens, eggs, fish, flesh, cattle, horses, sheep, geese, timber and boards. In 1571, an additional Swedish assessment was made on silverware, the register of which gives some indication of the relative wealth of the islanders. More than 1,000 farms were listed at the time, no fewer than sixty-two being operated by women.

E

The role of women in Ålandic farming is inseparable from the early development of commercial sea-going. Already by the end of the Middle Ages Ålanders were driving an active trade westwards to the towns around Lake Mälaren and eastwards beyond the Nyland coast to Reval and other Estonian ports. The winter *sumpar*—'swamps', as English travellers called the boats that carried the fish and other products swiftly to market—were about twice the size of the summer vessels. Ragna Ahlbäck (1955) discovered precise examples of the modest cargoes transported by two Kökar farmer traders. In the spring of 1624, Hans Mickelson carried on his Stockholm journey 3 barrels of potash and 4¾ barrels of salt fish, 6 sealskins, 3 calf skins, dried pike, eggs and game birds. In the autumn, Jens Olofsson took aboard 1 bullock, a cow, 2 sheep, a goat, 28 barrels of herring, 3 seal skins and a quantity of tallow. Frequently, the crews of the small trading vessels received the sacrament before sailing, and some carried a document from the local vicar guaranteeing their credentials. The autumn arrival of Ålandic fishermen—and, until very recently, their wives—on the quaysides of Stockholm, Helsinki, Åbo and other places, continues a centuries-old tradition.

> Who will buy my salmon,
> Perch, white fish or bream?
> Never among fish were such
>   fine fellows to be seen.
> Herring, can I oblige you with
> Barrels of them I will pack for you;
> Look, what thin tails and fat necks they have.

The Ålandic fishwives' chorus from Pacius's opera, long since forgotten by the musical world, still has echoes in the market place.

THE LANDSMAN AND THE SEAMAN

By the time record-keeping in Åland was being intensified, most of the cultivable land had been occupied and its uses well established. Pressure on the land was already evident by the end of the Middle Ages; it encouraged at an early stage the specialised use of different types of countryside, from the rock and rubble of the skerries, their plant colonies struggling with summer aridity as well as exposure, through the rich deciduous meadowlands, to the limited water meadows and lakeside grazings; from the scattered peat bogs through the broad arable claylands to the deciduous woodland grazings; from the moist spruce lands and the sandy heaths to the high crags. Pressure on the land also discouraged wasteful practices, such as woodland burning for cultivation. Because of the limited woodlands, pioneering, as experienced in the extensive forests of mainland Sweden and Finland, was rare in Åland. True enough, there was a thrust to the very margins of cultivable land in the earlier nineteenth century, but it was a different kind of colonisation. Åland's forests became private property at an early stage in historical times and little woodland was held in common. Local fuel and timber shortages have long been a problem.

Because of the complementary resources of the sea, the growing possibilities of escape to a life on the sea (naval as well as mercantile) and the eventual possibilities of emigration beyond the sea (with a corresponding retreat from more isolated and less rewarding settlements), interest in field and forest husbandry was never as strong as on the mainland. *Sjöbruk* —the use of the opportunities presented by the sea—usually took precedence over *landbruk*—the use of the opportunities presented by the land. The Ålander was temperamentally more seaman than landsman—his attitude pleasingly characterised by F. P. von Knorring: 'He sighs more deeply in the meadow under the heat of the sun than in the storm in danger on the sea.'

Partly because of this, Ålanders never experienced great difficulty in mustering the required number of sailors for the Swedish navy. Each of its semi-professional sailors (*båtsman*) had to be provided with a homestead (*torp*); the farm name Båtsmanstorp still persists in Åland. Such recruits to the Swedish navy were usually given succinct surnames. Admiralty lists of Ålanders in 1675 were dominanted by such descriptive monosyllabic names as Frisk (lively), Stark (strong), Snabb (quick), Brask (boastful), Svart (black), Vit (white), Grå (grey), Lång (long), Liten (little), as well as names of familiar creatures from the Åland skerries: Stut (bullock), Lärke (lark), Gök (cuckoo), Svala (swallow), Duva (dove).

Meanwhile, where families multiplied and farmland remained constant, limitations on land ownership forced many who took to the sea to undertake various forms of work obligation in exchange for a site on which to build their homes. These commitments were the humble counterparts of the day-work obligations required by the royal estates. Elis Karlsson (1964) recalls how they persisted into the late nineteenth century on the island of Vårdö.

In association with land taxation, Åland began to be mapped. Hans Hansson's *Åland och Sund Chartebok*, a collection of maps from the latter half of the seventeenth century, is the outstanding early example. It covers only a limited part of the archipelago, but contains some of the earliest large-scale maps of Finland. Consequently, with their aid it is possible to reconstruct the shape of particular farming communities as they existed three centuries ago. By the early eighteenth century, land surveyors were at work providing more up-to-date farm maps of parts of Åland. Among the more industrious of them was Engineer Wetterwijk, whose name appears on a succession of maps covering Saltvik parish between 1734 and 1752. These early maps focused upon the arable land, because this carried the highest taxation. Arable land, which was generally enclosed with wooden fences, was held in strips. Field names, in some cases already identifiable from the sixteenth century, had assumed firm forms by the eighteenth century. In the hamlet of Frebbenby in Hammarland, for example, each farm had fifty-six strips (or *tegar*) in the named fields. The strips were of varying size, the narrowest width being 10 *alnar* (approximately 9m) and the broadest, 32 *alnar*. The different bundles of strips in each of the three fields also bore their own descriptive names —*lertegar* (clay strips), *sandtegar* (sand strips), *brotegar* (strips by the bridge), and so on. The farms held woodland in three different areas and this was similarly divided.

Such communities were the object of continuing attention by Church authorities, who not only appointed parish priests, capable of giving practical as well as spiritual advice, but sent senior churchmen on formal visitations to inspect them. To Åland, for example, came Boetus Morenius on a series of visitations between 1637 and 1666. He was concerned not only with the fabrics of the church buildings and the vicarages, but with church attendance in the light of accessibility by road and by boat—a Scandinavian problem not confined to Åland—and with the general well-being and literacy of the communities. During his time the first Åland school came into being in Kvarnbo, Saltvik. In it, Latin lingered as a language of instruction well into the eighteenth century.

At a practical level, church and farm were linked through the church farm. Following the Reformation, many Lutheran clergy carried on the role of the Franciscan friars. Åland had no aristocracy of consequence, but in its well-to-do and generally active clergy it had a handful of men who were exemplars to the farming community. Saltvik church farm was fairly typical of the well-established holdings that were leading the rural communities in Åland by the later eighteenth century. It consisted of a dwelling house, two barns, a sheep pen, a shed for young cattle, a straw-thatched piggery, a brewing house with a well, a bakery with an oven, and a dairy. The buildings were hedged around with fruit bushes, cherry trees and a kitchen garden growing cabbages, potatoes, carrots and hops. Beyond the grainfields (the imported seed grains for which bore such exotic names as Mufti, Efendi, Wisir and Smirna) lay the grazing lands. It is scarcely surprising that there was insufficient fodder for the twelve cows, the bull, the fourteen calves, twenty-two sheep, four oxen and ten pigs, let alone the two horses (together with a foal) needed for the half-covered wagonette, the three chaises and the light and heavy sledges. In 1747, despite the effects of the invasion by Russian armies during 1742–3, Kumlinge vicarage supported even more stock. The inventory of livestock (all of which were appropriately clipped with the agreed earmarks) listed 115 animals, excluding dogs and cats. Among Åland's parish priests, personal effects matched in degree this array of live and dead stock.

It was such enlightened leaders of the community who encouraged the re-organisation of land holding (*Storskifte*) that was initiated by law from Stockholm in 1747. As with parliamentary enclosure in England, it was a highly desirable objective to create unified holdings out of the scattered possessions of most farms. But the theory did not always fit the practice, and the exercise that increased the efficiency of farm holdings and produced such excellent maps was a prolonged and litigious business. Quite small parcels of land might take six or seven years to re-allocate; an entire hamlet took five times as long. It was a part of the Ålandic social scene recorded by some of the foreign travellers. One English visitor considered the surveyors to do 'more mischief than twice their number of publicans in England'.

TOPOGRAPHICAL VIEWS

The age of topography to which these observations belonged produced both domestic and foreign views of Åland. The first brief topographical account of Åland was written in Latin—*De Alandia, Maris Baltici Insula* (Uppsala, 1739, 1745). In it, Christopherus Tärnström presented the islands in a classical posture as interceding with Neptune. The second sprang out of medical ground. The post of medical practitioner to the province was established in 1778 and Frederic Wilhelm Radloff was appointed to it in 1789; he published his description of Åland in 1795. Central to it was a review of the population of the archipelago. As with the rest of Sweden and Finland, a population census of Åland had been taken at regular intervals from 1750. In 1790, the average household consisted of eight or nine persons and the 11,400 population consisted principally of *bönder*, or owner-farmers, who combined fishing and farming. There were twenty priests, fifteen civil servants and twenty-eight others (such as bridgemen) in public pay, 103 boatmen and sixty-five pilots. The pilot service had already been well developed by the end of the Swedish period, boys being encouraged to learn the art of pilotage from their fathers. It was a measure of the self-sufficiency of the rural community that the occupation census listed only sixty-two craftsmen of various kinds. Some, like tailors, were itinerant. At the same time, the annual production of 22,500 barrels of grain indicated a deficiency which had to be made up by imports. This raised no problems in peace time, but it made for difficulties when war interrupted trading. In general, Åland lay outside the famine zone of Scandinavia; but infant mortality was high and cold could take its toll of the under-nourished. 'Frozen to death' was a cause of mortality not uncommonly listed.

Edward Clarke, who travelled to Scandinavia with Thomas Malthus, came to Finland by way of Åland in the high winter of 1799. The arctic world of Åland—less than 1,000km from London as the crow flies—made a powerful impression upon him. Joseph Acerbi, Sir Robert Ker Porter and Sir John Bowring had much the same initiation. Sir Robert declared that Ulysses never encountered so many perils among the islands of the Syrens as he experienced in the Åland Islands—and, at least, he added, Ulysses had agreeable women. For Acerbi, the hazards of the 'immense chaos of icy ruins' in which the Åland Sea was fixed were multiplied by horses terrified by the scent of his wolf and bearskin pelisses. Edward Clarke was struck by the hardiness and endurance of the Åland women folk—how they helped their husbands on uncomfortable sleigh journeys, sometimes working deep in ice water; how they enjoyed the general revels after the church service when, hair smoothed with beer and decorated with beads, they cracked their whips above the spike-shod horses and played the part of female charioteers. The seal hunters impressed Edward Clarke with their bravery and cunning; so, too, did those who operated the post boats. Clarke experienced life in the raw. Al fresco midwinter meals consisted of bread 'looking like a sugar loaf' which had to be broken with a hammer, roast game which was cut up like a snowball, and wine which sometimes froze in the bottle. Worse was yet to come at Vårdö post house, where the naked company slept in bunks, one above another, as in a ship's cabin, and breakfast began, even for the babies, with a dram of firewater.

Most travellers who followed the post route through Åland saw it in summer when the ferrymen's tariffs were at the lowest. They might even sit in their chairs on the ferry boats and build up their idylls of the islands. For Thomas Malthus, in 1800, all teemed with natural beauty, and his cockleshell boat passed sleek cattle swimming from islet to islet to glean grass. Sir Robert Ker Porter had also heard of these amphibious cattle and had visions of 'the damsels' of the household taking a trip 'in the European fashion' on their adventurous backs. Sir John Carr viewed the islands as 'just such a spot as the poetical spirit of Cowper would have coveted'. For the French, L. Léouzon le Duc presented the Åland sun in its mild summer sky as 'une lampe enfermée dans un globe d'opale'. No other voices disturbed the tranquil atmosphere than those of fishermen singing their sea songs; no other sounds than those of the nets as they were cast into the water for fish.

But by this time, ordinary Ålanders were beginning to record their daily life for themselves. Among them was Henrik August Wenström, a Seglinge farmer who kept a six-month journal of his daily activities. During May and June, his time was occupied principally by fishing (with ordinary nets and bow nets), ditch digging, fencing, clearing a small piece of new ground, carpentry and journeys to fetch supplies and provisions. In early July before the hay harvest, he put up 'wedding posts' outside his home for a family marriage. By mid-July, haymaking ousted other activities. It took place on a number of different parcels of land from which it had to be transported by human labour, since the horse was put out to grass on 21 June. The first two weeks of August were spent entirely in cutting bundles of twigs to be dried as leaf fodder. In the third week of August, the grain harvest began. Threshing and grain drying followed before the return to fishing and the despatch of a rich daily harvest by the *sump* boats *Cecilia, Leo* and *North Star* to Stockholm. In October came the potato harvest, grain milling, twig cutting (for fuel), barrel-making (for autumn herrings) and trapping. Henrik paid strict adherence to the Sabbath and, if there was no church journey, it was recorded as a day of rest. It may be calculated that Henrik spent 31 per cent of his time in activities associated with fishing; 18 per cent cultivating his land; 19 per cent harvesting; 16 per cent on handicrafts and 16 per cent on journeys. Livestock, horses apart, did not engage his attention; they were the prerogative of his wife.

THE CLIMAX OF SELF-SUFFICIENCY

Features of the near self-sufficient household in the near self-sufficient community lingered to within living memory. They were more persistent in the outlying parishes. It was a life rooted in a rocky land but succoured generously by the sea. Most people lived in rough-hewn log dwellings, until steam saw mills produced cheap planks. Above the cluster of farm buildings needed to accommodate animals in winter rose the wooden sails of windmills. Life centred in large living rooms, whose capacious brick or stone ovens were only slowly replaced by cast-iron stoves and kitchen ranges. Small windows looked

on to a scatter of pocket-handkerchief fields which produced a
scarcely adequate harvest of grain (certainly insufficient to
keep chickens), potatoes, peas (which were dried) and vegetables. Grazing animals were kept out of the hay lands and had
to seek food from the boulder-ridden woodlands, the edge of
the boglands and the reed pastures that fringed the shore.
Traditional work rhythms were most evident at haytime and
harvest. Haymaking started first in the skerries and then shifted
to the home meadows, the whole family scything and carrying
bundles—in fish nets, on the back, on litters and by boat. The
day's work began at 5 am, with breakfast at 10. After an hour's
rest, work continued until late evening. At the time of the rye
harvest, men and women worked together, the former sickling
and the latter binding. Threshing and winnowing were usually
done by four people together.

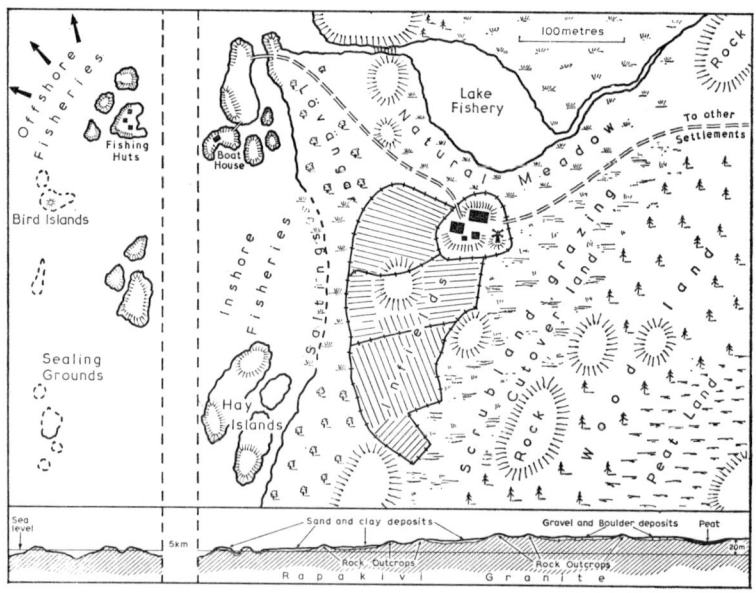

Components of a nineteenth-century Åland homestead

The harvest from the sea compensated for the shortcomings of the land. In the offshore fisheries there were commonly three nettings of fish a day—at dawn, at midday and in the evening. They took place from the fishing camps in the outer skerries. The content as well as the rhythm of meals had become fixed by the later nineteenth century—the early morning coffee and sandwiches, the midday meal of herring, the evening meal of cods' heads. If bad weather prevented cod fishing, the customary fare was salted herring stewed in sour milk with marjoram; it was called 'storm soup'. The secrets of the offshore fisheries were transmitted almost ritualistically to the next generation. Sometimes they were recorded in so-called *torskböcker* (codfish books) or *torskbiblar* (codfish bibles). A splendid example, dated 1828, is Eric Österlund's book from Skinnarsen in Kökar archipelago. The book identifies (for the long-sighted in clear weather) the art of fixing by landmarks the location of the celebrated Möskär fishing grounds. Along the inshore waters, the location of bow nets acquired established patterns. In winter, net fishing took place through holes in the ice.

In late winter, seal hunting reached a climax. Groups of ten to fifteen hunters armed with harpoons, clubs and knives, participated in the arduous assault on the seal colonies. Nets were also used, especially around seal holes. In summer, there was a limited amount of shooting. At the end of the eighteenth century, the seal hunt yielded about 3,000 a year. As with fishing grounds, sealing grounds were regarded as private property.

So, too, was the third feature of the coastal economy, the bird colony. Egg and down collecting grounds, as well as netting districts, were clearly understood by custom and the law of trespass applied to them. The eider duck enjoyed protection at an early stage in Åland's history and it was forbidden to take its eggs. Eider duck apart, the shooting season lasted from the end of March until mid-May. During the season, large numbers of plucked birds were salted down.

In the self-sufficient economy, the skills of ploughwright, boat-builder, mason, miller, smith, carpenter, cobbler and tailor were frequently vested in a handful of men. While all respected property rights, the fixed and moveable goods that they constructed commonly bore individual signs, or *bomärken*, in the same way that animals were earmarked. Some of Åland's marks, such as the hacked cross, are of considerable antiquity.

The community had to cope in sickness as well as in health. The solitary apothecary on the main island was only of limited help, so the assistance of leeches was regularly sought and the cupping horns, in which there was so much belief, can still be found. Traditional remedies for rheumatic pains were horse-radish leaves, birch leaves and pine needles; for stomach troubles, *Artimesia absinthium*; for swellings, *Polytrichium*; for wounds, *Lycoperdon* (puff balls), mixed with salt and brandy; for throat troubles, black currant or camomile; for lung inflammation, the inevitable tar water.

The meagre and somewhat monotonous fare that character-ised everyday meals looked basically to rye until the coming of milled grains in the mid-nineteenth century. Rye meal was also mixed with fish, fowl, liver, seal's blood or bird fat and smoked in sausage casings. Mushrooms and fresh berries added seasonal variation. Christmas was the social climax of the year. It was anticipated by the brewing of special ale ('dark as blood', as one observer put it), by the making of long tallow candles (to put into the branched candelabras that stood on the tables), by a three or four day baking session (with yeast bread supplementing the usual black bread and sour bread), by the preparation of special fish soups, and by house-cleaning and bathing. The sleigh journey to the Christmas services might take several hours and began soon after midnight. Afterwards, the traditional Scandinavian meal of pike and rice porridge was eaten. Coffee, widely established by the end of the eighteenth century, was drunk. The Christmas tree made its appearance in Åland in the 1850s and a decade later the custom of giving presents was introduced. Skate and ski, which most children knew how to use by the age of five or six, added their contribution to the Christmas atmosphere.

In retrospect and expressed in this way, it sounds a picturesque existence. As recorded in the *genre* paintings of Karl Emanuel Jansson (1846–74), it has a homely appeal. But it was only the better-off farmers who followed it. Åland, like Finland at large, had large numbers of virtually landless crofters (*torpare*) and fishermen whose life was pitched in a lower key and crowded into the cramped living space of small wooden cottages. Some idea of the scant possessions of the crofters can be gleaned from wills which are available from the period 1850–1900; of the 8,600 extant documents, nearly a quarter were filed by crofters. The most valuable of their humble possessions in most cases was a solitary cow. For the family of the crofter, the sea provided an even more important outlet than for most. It was an activity given new impetus by sailing privileges accorded by Russia after 1856, which permitted Åland traders to move beyond the Baltic Sea.

THE SMALL-SCALE CARRYING TRADE

By the time that the traditional features of Ålandic life and labour were being recorded, sea-going activity was assuming new shape. One of the most distinctive characteristics was the development of the so-called *bondeseglation*—small-scale, cooperatively sponsored carrying trade. The easing of international carrying restrictions, the rising demand for commodities, the elimination of the tolls in the Danish Sound in 1857—all encouraged Ålanders to move outside the Baltic. In 1856, the first Åland ship sailed beyond the Kattegat. In 1865, *Preciosa*, from Eckerö, was the first Åland vessel to cross the Atlantic; its logbook is still in immaculate condition. The development of shipping in the parish of Lemland is beautifully illustrated in a succession of maps prepared by David Papp

THE ÅLAND ISLANDS

(1971) in his study of Åland's navigation, 1800–1940. In 1842, Lemland trading vessels were confined to the Bothnian Sea and the Stockholm-Åbo axis. By 1852, they had established connections with the north German ports; by 1862, all the principal Danish ports were visited and the first British links established; by 1872, British connections were strong and a Belgian contact had been made; by 1882, French and Belgian connections were as numerous as British.

The fleet that engaged in this trade consisted of wooden ships of several hundred tons burden, manned with a crew of ten or twelve. Because of the form of ownership, it could be said of Ålanders 100 years ago that there was scarcely anyone who had not a ship to think about. A letter to the newspaper *Åbo Underrättelser*, dated 19 February 1867, identified one Åland ship which was owned cooperatively by a miscellaneous group of thirty-two shareholders, including builders, postilions, cooks and loggers. Complementarily, the wills of deceased Ålanders give an indication of the distribution of shares held; that of Bonden Johan Erik Lundberg, of Granboda in Lemland, is representative. On his death, he owned shares in schooners as follows: $\frac{1}{8}$ in *Frederika*, $\frac{1}{16}$ in *Leo*, $\frac{1}{10}$ in *Primus*, $\frac{1}{16}$ in *Celia*, $\frac{1}{16}$ in *Eli*, $\frac{1}{16}$ in *Furstalen*, $\frac{3}{28}$ in *Matilda*. The village of Vargata in Vårdö was an apotheosis of the Ålandic situation. Its residents had twenty-six trading vessels in the 1860s. In 1875, Vårdö had 6·8 tons of shipping per capita. Beyond these interests there were the interests of the ship builders themselves, for many vessels were of local provenance. Bambölevik was typical of the near anonymous, but active little wharves that slipped into the sea its quota of vessels—*Adina, Adonis, Agda, Aglaja* being its best-known alliterative quartet.

The carrying trade was competitive with farming. In the first place, this was because ships represented a considerable proportion of Åland's limited capital investment; Georg Kåhre has estimated that in the mid-nineteenth century Åland had three tons of shipping for every acre of cultivated land. In the second place, there was seasonal competition for farm labour and, thirdly, ships' captains were not infrequently farmers who left their wives at home to keep the farm in order. Some idea of the situation is provided by Lemland parish in the mid-1870s, which had only 350 men between the ages of fifteen and fifty, yet listed 340 seamen in its occupational returns. Trade was conducted principally between the Baltic and European Atlantic ports. In the 1860s, there were no fewer than 200 ships on the English run alone. Journeys from Bothnian harbours to Channel ports rarely took less than three weeks and frequently over five; it is said that the Åland skipper's dream was a three-week trip to England. At this rate, even a good return journey took six to eight weeks, so that, given an open season of somewhat more than six months, three or four round trips were about as many as were possible. Some ships stayed in the Mediterranean during the winter. Most were hauled up for tarring, oiling, keel scraping, smithing and sail repair.

Shipping was a hazardous business and Ålanders availed themselves increasingly of marine insurance after the opening of the Åbo office in 1865. Not surprisingly, insurance agents insisted on greater precautions; in particular, they pressed for the better charting, marking and lighting of the Ålandic coasts. Despite losses, profits from trading were large and transformed the living standards of many.

The growth in material wealth was evident in domestic furnishing and appurtenances, in jewellery and 'thick gold rings' that enabled seamen to capture 'the loyalty of their housewives' (as an Åland priest put it), above all in the dwelling houses themselves. The gradual expansion of many Ålandic farmhouses, big out of all proportion to their surrounding farmland, has its roots in the profitable carrying trade. Such dwellings were the antithesis of the cramped and uncomfortable conditions at sea. Pellas, the Lemland farmhouse described by Pamela Eriksson, is typical of them—with its 'iron-hard pin pine beams, fourteen-inch-wide flooring planks . . . and thousands of feet of lapping boards'. Soon, such sturdy timbers were to be exhausted and Ålanders had slowly to turn to other constructional materials. Kökar builders found an unusual and cheaper material than granite blocks out of which to construct house foundations—the dark green, glossy bricks made from the slag of mainland furnaces, such as Dahlsbruk.

To the same period belongs the foundation of the port of Mariehamn. Requests for the establishment of a trading centre in Åland had been put to the Swedish authorities on a number of occasions in the eighteenth century. Godby in Finström, Flaka in Lemland and Yternäs in Jomala had all been proposed as possible sites. It had been increasingly irksome for Åland's trade to pass through the customs houses of Stockholm or Åbo. In 1859, Alexander II agreed that a port and market centre should be created at Övernäs; it was named Mariehamn, after his empress.

THE END OF AN ERA

The settlement of Åland reached a climax towards the end of the nineteenth century. The scattered communities, the sites of whose homesteads had known human habitation since before recorded history, had struck a stable balance between arable and meadow, forest and *löväng*. Around the coast, any harbour which commanded fishing grounds had its handful of fisher-farmers' dwellings with sturdy boathouses for pinewood craft and home-made gear. It was a pattern not uncommon to those of most Scandinavian archipelagos. Already visitors were finding in its humble activities and relaxed rhythms an appealing harmony and security. Across the Åland Sea, the restless August Strindberg discovered a measure of repose in the life of the Stockholm skerries and immortalised it in his novelette, *The People of Hemsö*. Åland had no literary counterpart to transfigure its skerry modes and manners, but it had its summer visitors. Among them was Greta Westerholm, whose period pieces recall the social pattern of late nineteenth-century villa

Page 89 (*above*) The town hall of Mariehamn where the parliament of Åland holds its sessions until a special building for local administration is completed; (*below*) Mariehamn: a view of the main shopping street. During the season shops and department stores are busy with tourists. The former character of Mariehamn is mostly lost today with the disappearance of wooden houses with small gardens

Page 90 (left) The medieval church at Finström framed by oak and ash leaves, a traditional slat-rail fence and a restored windmill; (below) logging operations in Åland

life. Åland has also found enthusiasts such as Gösta Tallquist, who recorded the new stirrings in the rural community that led to the establishment of Åland's first folk high school in Finström in 1895 and the foundation of the farmers' association (*Lantmanna Förening*) in 1886. Simultaneously, the early days of the carrying trade, which had done so much to stimulate the Ålander mentally and to benefit him materially, were coming to an end. Some regard this sea-going episode as synonymous with the first boom in Åland's economic life. The memories that it left behind, drained of their difficulties and refined of their dross, were those of a golden age.

6　A CROSSROADS OF THE BALTIC

As a part of the buffer territory between eastern and western Europe, Åland has suffered a succession of invasions and occupations. Once Russia had established its window on the Baltic, pressure on the eastern foreland increased. The simultaneous decline in Swedish authority exposed the vulnerability of Finland. In 1709–21 (during the Great Northern Wars); in 1742–3; in 1808–9 (during the Napoleonic wars), and in 1854–5 (during the Baltic naval campaigns of the Crimean War), the Åland Islands experienced the direct effects of military action. In 1914–18 and 1939–44, the inhabitants of the islands were subject to indirect pressures and uncertainties. The reactions of the Ålanders to these successive crises in their history have changed as they have become more numerous, more articulate and more ethnographically conscious.

THE GREAT NORTHERN WAR

Physical occupation by Russian troops occurred for the first time during the Great Northern Wars. Occupation was inseparable from the fact that the Åland Islands formed the western extremity of the principal Finnish axis of communications and the bridgehead to metropolitan Sweden. The ferry and post route from the Swedish port of Grisslehamn to the fortress outpost of Wiborg (the Finnish Viipuri) at the head of the Finnish Gulf embraced the Åland archipelago as its first stage. The map on p 124 illustrates the route as it can be reconstructed from F. W. Radloff's description of Åland from 1795.

The response of many Ålanders during the Great Northern War was to withdraw from the area of Russian occupation. Not all of the archipelago was occupied all of the time, and some of it was never disturbed, but settlement was concentrated along the post route and most Ålanders consequently suffered harassment. Settlements from Brändö in the east, through Kumlinge, Vårdö and Åland mainland, to Eckerö in the west were burned and pillaged. Sund and Vårdö were the parishes that seem to have suffered most. In summer, ships of the Russian navy—including galleys manned with oarsmen—patrolled the labyrinthine channels. Peter the Great was himself with the fleet in Flaka harbour, off south Lemland, in 1719. During winter, troops quartered on the islands made forays across the frozen channels. Rather more than a fifth of Åland's 5,000 inhabitants eventually left the occupied lands, either for mainland Sweden or for the remoter parts of the archipelago. The movements of some of the evacuees can be traced from the communion books which the priests carried with them. Valdemar Nyman, in his romantic novel *Den stora flykten*, traces the flight of one fictional refugee, Johannes Lilienwahn, to symbolise all flight. A few Ålanders took to the traditional hiding places in caves, such as Kloddstugan in Bertby and Djupvik 'church' in Geta. There was some partisan activity; Stefan Löving's diary from 1710–20 recounts the experiences of one of the local guerillas. Partisans often found greater satisfaction than those who heeded the general call to arms only to find inadequate training and insufficient weapons.

Åland provided the setting for elaborate, but unsuccessful, peace negotiations in 1719. They were conducted at Vårdö, on the post route, partly because it had the best available buildings, though many farms were robbed of their roofing materials, doors and windows to produce the additional accommodation needed for the several hundred people who gathered on the scene. A sea battle off Flisö in Föglö in July 1720, commonly called the battle of Ledsund, heralded the end of the conflict.

93

Stability was restored to the islands by the Treaty of Nystad which formally concluded the Great Northern Wars in 1721. Recuperation was slow. The time of 'general poverty and lamentation', as it was described, was exacerbated by a succession of hard winters and cold summers. Finström church book recorded cold so severe that 'people suffered injury to hands, feet and faces'. Food, fodder and shelter were all short. Population drifted slowly back to restore the derelict hamlets and to reclaim the overgrown fields. In the absence of draught animals, the spade replaced the plough. Animal stocks could only be slowly replaced. It was not easy to build up a stock such as that lost by the owner of Södergård in Lövö—two horses, thirteen cows, one three-year-old bullock, six at two years old, six at one year old, five calves, sixteen old ewes, fourteen young ones, sixteen lambs, ten she-goats, seven bucks, six pigs and seven chickens. There were other losses—from the considerable stands of oak woods, removed by the invaders to prevent their subsequent use by the Swedish fleet, to the elimination of the royal elk stocks. To the small communities, with so many other tasks on hand, the restoration of the medieval churches—in three cases reduced to stone shells—made formidable demands. Not much remains from 'the Great Wrath', as the episode is known in Scandinavian history; though a reconnaissance by underwater archaeologists has located at least thirteen wrecks from the battle of Ledsund.

THE LITTLE NORTHERN WAR

Less than a generation later, a further Swedo-Russian conflict impinged on Åland. Although Swedish troops were sent to protect the archipelago, they had little success. In the autumn of 1742, the familiar pattern of retreat and migration was repeated. The sea passage to Sweden had to be undertaken in equinoctial gales. Many lost belongings and not a few their lives in stormy crossings. Animals were transported by the hundred, church bells and plate were shipped in the company of brandy kegs and stills. Nils Mattson, of Ytterby in Jomala, listed the worldly goods that he lost on the high seas—silver, copper and iron ware, clothes and bed linen, fishing nets and gear. Pilots fled from the islands under threat of Russian impressment; men aged eighteen to thirty-six were drafted into the Swedish naval service. Those who stayed behind, and they included many older people and servants, had to swear fealty to the Empress Catherine. But there remained plenty of local opposition, so that harassment of Russian encampments by bands of Ålanders continued throughout the occupation. Following the Peace of Åbo, families again returned to their neglected homesteads, while carpenters, glaziers and smiths were called upon to restore the desecrated churches. The Russians left behind a scatter of stone-built ovens (called locally *ryssugnar*) which had been used for baking bread. These curious relics of the eighteenth-century campaigns, deceptively prehistoric in appearance, may still be seen around Ledsund.

THE NAPOLEONIC WAR

Experiences during the war of 1808–9 were harder and more is known about them. They were set against the background of an unusually severe winter, so that it was possible, in January 1809, to cross from Åland to the Swedish as well as to the Finnish mainland. The collapse of Swedish resistance in Finland left the way open for Russian occupation of Åland and the use of the archipelago as a base for assault upon Sweden proper. In the first stages of the battle, Swedish and Russian troops skirmished to and fro over the islands. In the summer of 1808, Gustaf Adolf IV came himself with troops to Finström, tried to move to the Finnish mainland, but was forced back to Lemland in October. In order to render the eastern archipelago useless to the invaders, the retreating Swedish army systematically evacuated the inhabitants and destroyed any useful buildings in

Kumlinge, Brändö and Sottunga parishes. The evacuees were moved to Geta and Hammarland. No fewer than 128 properties were pulled down, some being fired by the owners themselves. Timber stocks were put into the sea. Straw and fodder were burned if they could not be removed. Movable goods, church furnishings and foodstuffs were carried away. If animals could not be transported, they were slaughtered and roasted for the troops. Meanwhile, from other parts of Åland, professional people and those who were better off moved to the mainland. Naval records list the substantial number of Åland recruits who entered the Swedish service.

The 'Swedish Fire' (*Svenska elden*), as it was known, was succeeded by the 'Russian Fire'. As many as 17,000 Russians are presumed to have participated in the Åland campaign. Following their occupation of the archipelago, arms, ammunition and flints had to be given up and allegiance sworn to the tsar. Disease followed invasion, and at least 30 per cent of the Ålanders succumbed. Eventually, in March 1809, the Swedish army made a retreat across the ice to Grisslehamn. This episode was among a number that created a legend around the ingenuity and humanity of the Swedish General von Döbeln. A monument was erected to his memory on Signildskär, from which he sledded his sick and wounded over the ice to the Swedish shore, protected by four corner columns along a staked route.

The Treaty of Fredrikshamn (F. Hamina) brought peace to an archipelago which Sweden agreed to renounce for ever. The displaced islanders returned home with passports to a part of the Grand Duchy of Russia. The losses that they had suffered were speedily assessed. Compensation was received from both King Gustaf and the Tsar Alexander—kroner mixed with kopeks. Approximately 3,500 Ålanders acquired a new allegiance to the Russian tsar when representatives of Finland swore fealty in Borgå (F. Porvoo) cathedral in 1809, following the Peace of Fredrikshamn.

A CROSSROADS OF THE BALTIC

Having acquired an extended front on the Baltic, it was not long before Russia felt the need to establish a defence system on its westernmost approaches, of which Åland was now a part. In the 1830s in the parish of Sund, commanding Lumpar Bay and within comfortable distance of the ruined medieval Kastelholm, the Russians set about building a major fortress with outlying bunkers which was christened Bomarsund. Adjacent to it, the little civilian settlement of Skarpans grew up. The author of John Murray's first guide to Finland, published in 1839, introduced Bomarsund to British travellers as having 'room within its extensive ramparts for upwards of 60,000 men and a harbour capable of containing the whole Russian fleet'. It was this fortress which was to familiarise western Europe with the name of Åland and to bring to its shores for the first time tens of thousands of British and French.

THE ÅLAND WAR

Although Crimea gave its name to the conflict between Russia, Britain and France that developed in 1854, there were also related naval campaigns in the Baltic Sea. The purpose of the British and French naval expeditions to the Baltic during the summers of 1854 and 1855 was to destroy as many as possible of the Russian fortifications at the approaches to St Petersburg. Among these, the outermost were the most vulnerable—the newly constructed fortress at Bomarsund in Åland and the old-established stronghold of Sveaborg (F. Suomenlinna) at the gateway to Helsinki. A subsidiary operation was to destroy the stocks of naval stores, principally tar and pitch, at Finnish ports. Success in these operations called for control of Ålandic waters—more precisely, summer control, for the naval campaigns were exclusively summer campaigns cut short by the first smell of autumn frost. Their objective to blockade the coast of Russia could therefore be only partially achieved.

Ålandic waters were virtually unknown to the British.

97

Although the major leads had been plotted two generations earlier, adequate charts for Admiral Sir Charles Napier's fleet were unavailable. So treacherous were the channels of the islands that the first Finnish passenger ships, running from Stockholm to St Petersburg by way of the islands, anchored by night. 'The Baltic was . . . to the ships of the navy almost a *mare ignotum*', wrote a contributor to *Blackwood's Magazine*. For old sailors, to enter Ålandic waters was like 'putting your head in a sack'. A successful assault on Bomarsund called for pilots with a personal knowledge of the waters.

And pilots were not to be found. The British minister in Stockholm wrote to Sir Charles Napier, in April 1854, that the Russians 'had taken all the boats on shore and some way up into the country and they have moved not only all the buoys and lighthouses but the pilots who live on the coasts'. Swedish pilots apparently knew little of Åland. The services of a few were eventually obtained, though the Finnish authorities put a price on their heads for capture or death. But even such pilots could not guarantee a safe passage for vessels of a size to which they were unaccustomed—certainly not to shipping drawing over 6m.

The log books from ships of the Baltic fleet are consequently scattered with references to vessels grounding, sticking fast, stripping off their copper sheathing and even bursting their bows. So men-of-war 'crawled about with leadsmen' and were preceded by rowing boats from which sailors plumbed the depths. 'Keep the leads going', was the order of the day. Of the *Leopard*, a wit commented that she had some 'honourable spots . . . on her bottom' as well as on her side. Nor was communication with the Ålanders an easy matter. Interpreters had to be found—and handsomely paid at fifteen to twenty shillings a day. At least it was discovered through them that the Bomarsund garrison contained no more than 1,500–2,000 men. Åland's climate was equally a mystery to the navy. The severity of the Baltic winter was legendary. Swedish fleets, from those of Sten

A CROSSROADS OF THE BALTIC

Sture to those of Gustavus III, were known to have been trapped in the ice. The freezing and break-up of ice and its duration were phenomena but little understood. 'The month of September in the Baltic corresponds in severity with November here or in the Channel Islands,' wrote a correspondent to *The Times*. The *Illustrated London News* in 1854 scarcely cheered naval authorities by reproducing a sketch of a frigate draped in autumn icicles to illustrate the problem. 'Rolling masses of half sunken ice' also delayed action until well into the spring. The navy had no intention of sitting out the rigours of the Baltic as the army sat out those of the Crimea, though the possibility of assembling 'skating battalions' for a possible winter attack was considered in 1854. Contrastingly, the navy in Ålandic waters was surprised at the intensity of the summer heat. Awnings were spread over the decks and men took to their white duck trousers.

In one respect, by comparison with the British naval visits to the Baltic in 1811–12, manoeuvrability in and around Åland's coasts was eased. Steam supported sail. Admiral Napier's fleet of sixteen vessels consisted of battleships and frigates driven by paddle-wheels and screws. But, although the steam engine enabled ships to sail where they wished in spite of contrary winds, regular coaling was called for. So, to Ålandic waters came colliers from more than 1,000 miles away, carrying several hundred tons apiece of smokeless Welsh fuels. In order to economise on coal, vessels not infrequently towed each other. Timber was also burned in their boilers. Each unit of the fleet had its particular purpose—smaller, swifter ships to chase vessels attempting to run the blockade and big men-of-war for direct assault.

To Bomarsund came some of the most splendid British ships of the line. They included three-decker vessels bristling with over 100 cannon and each manned by 1,000 men. 'The stone forts of Russia are no match for the floating batteries of England and France,' declared *The Times*, after the demise of Bomar-

99

sund. But there were anxious moments before the eventual attack. Officers were apprehensive of ambush in the narrow channels. Screens or hammocks were erected over the decks in case a battery attacked the ships at close range. As for casualties, a British newspaper, anxious for action, wryly commented: 'they are some of the most beautiful ships in the world and we cannot afford to lose them.'

The reactions of members of the fleet and of those who followed in its wake to the Åland Islands was mixed. For the artist, Oswald Brierly, who produced such splendid coloured lithographs from the arena of activities, the 14km sail from Ledsund to Bomarsund was a pastoral idyll—'small farms with cattle and cornfields, windmills and the occasional peep of a homely-looking church'. The great line-of-battle ships that went rushing past, darkening the air with their dense clouds of smoke, provided a strange contrast. Among the fleet followers was a sporting don from Magdalen College, Oxford, the Reverend J. W. Hughes, who came in his 10-ton yacht to watch the campaign. Parts of Åland reminded him of Barnstaple and Mount Edgecombe in England. The *United Services Gazette* (12 August 1854) presented a less appealing picture: 'the desolate appearance of the coast, the . . . sombre verdure of the firs . . . on the sides of the rock a few wretched cabins built of wood dried up by the cold and the sun'. Rock ruled—'you would think an earthquake had forced it up out of the bowels of the earth,' was the observation in the *Illustrated London News*. It was 'execrable ground' over which to haul guns and cannon, yet the Rev Hughes reported the lusty singing of the 150-strong teams of naval ratings who heaved them over rock and boulder.

The Ålanders accepted the intruders with equanimity. Hughes found the housewives more interested in their cows than in the soldiery, while their daughters were 'of native innocence'. Both offered gifts of strawberries and wild fruit to the British and French, but when it came to essentials, such as fresh meat, the market price prevailed, as the Ålandic price list published in the *Illustrated London News* attested. Fresh water was fetched from local streams, some of which remained in local terminology, 'English brooks'.

Within bugle call of Bomarsund, the British and French pitched their camps picturesquely framed by 'pines which still drooped in August from last winter's burden of snow'. Hughes observed that the ever-ingenious sappers 'had built themselves the neatest little huts of small fir branches', while the officers 'had a splendid bell tent as big as a bullock shed'. Life appears to have been a long *fête champêtre*—'picnic and cricket parties were frequent'. Sketching and painting were in the highest fashion; Captain Keith Stewart's sketch book provides an outstanding example. Midshipmen wrote home for sketch books (letters cost officers sixpence and ratings fivepence); the artistic abilities of some seamen excited the envy of their superiors. The Rev Hughes noted an artist at Fort Tzee 'arranging his drawing material as much at home as if he had been at Hyde Park or Hampstead'.

Afloat, there were amateur theatricals, with the quarterdeck of the flagship converted into an auditorium. And, as might be expected, the French produced gustatory miracles. Trading vessels were not slow to realise the commercial potential of occupied Åland and ensured an adequate supply of victuals, as well as 'French brandy and Dutch porter for thirsty souls', as Hughes reported it. Lolling in the calm waters, the merchantmen were sitting targets for an enemy who appeared indifferent to the morale induced by their vital cargoes.

At home, the prospect of the assault on Åland's fortress stirred excited support. Imaginative panoramas, such as that by Mr Packer of the storming of Bomarsund, were printed before the event took place. To the basic ingredients of fortress and toppling pines were added encircling hills and peaks of Scottish dimensions. Simultaneously, adventurous holidaymakers embarked upon excursions to the impending scene of the battle. They even advertised in the press—'desirous of visiting the scene of operations . . . would join in hiring a crew's steamer to proceed and attend the motions of the fleet'. Other sightseers came from Stockholm. The event occasioned a series of cartoons, by F. L. von Dardel, showing the Tutting family and its pleasure trip to see the allied fleet in Bomarsund.

Apart from the theatrical spectacle of the fleet 'dressed in their colours and with bands playing', the eventual attack on Bomarsund was something of an anti-climax. In Britain and France, the public had expected an event which would eclipse Sevastopol. Instead, as Admiral Napier wrote succinctly to his daughter, Fanny, on 16 August 1854, 'Bomarsund . . . surrendered without a fight'. But, if no light brigades charged, plenty of cannon engaged in preliminary volleying and thundering, and E. T. Dolby produced plenty of dramatic sketches of naval incidents for popular consumption. There were many different impressions of the fall of Bomarsund. The press trumpeted a great victory. Napoleon III struck a splendid medal. The *Army and Navy Gazette* (26 August 1854) chided the pacifist opposition that 'the veriest humanity monger of the Peace Society cannot find fault with the assault on Bomarsund.' Mr Punch had his sick joke by looking at the event from the Russian angle— Corporal Kickumoff with his ten men and their one gun sinking ten units of the allied fleet. Felix Karlsson, an Ålander reminiscing in 1904, recalled that, when the Finnish troops were ordered to open the main gate of the fortress, they replied 'If *they* cannot open it, they can stay outside.' The event provided additional folklore for Finland in general and Åland in particular. Above all, it gave rise to a stirring song, known to Finns as *Oolanin sota*—the Åland War. It recalls how a handful of Finns in their humble fishing boats scattered the English fleet and Åland emerged victorious.

Åland, indeed, did emerge victorious, though in a different and rather more fundamental way. First of all, it was physically demilitarised; finally, it was demilitarised by international agreement. To start with, some 2,000 prisoners of war were taken and divided between the British and the French—Admiral Napier claiming a head tax on them! After the prisoners had boarded the transports and the Ålanders had removed the stores and provisions from the fortress, Bomarsund was systematically destroyed by British and French sappers. Today, the ruins round the grassy spaces of its great parade ground have decayed and matured sufficiently to take on a picturesque quality. They are not exactly an Ålandic shrine, but they provide an effective, if unlikely, setting for a summer theatre. The events which reduced them to rubble are a forgotten chapter in European history.

The prisoners were taken to England and France where they had their own extraordinary experiences. Among trophies brought to the Tower of London was the bell of Skarpans church; it was eventually returned to the new church designed by Lars Sonck for Mariehamn. Burial places are scattered around Lumpar Bay; some carrying memorials to more than 100 allied troops killed before the white flag was hoisted. On Fjälskär, for example, one commemorates George Privett and Thomas Barker from HMS *Penelope*. On Prästö there are small graveyards—Orthodox, Protestant, Catholic, Jewish and Mohammedan—recalling the soldiers in the Russian army who died while on service in the fortress.

WORLD WAR I

As tension in the Baltic arena mounted during World War I, Åland was drawn unwittingly into the limelight. Although neutralised and demilitarised by international agreement, this detached and most vulnerable part of the Grand Duchy of Finland gave rise to Russian apprehension. Already, in the early years of the twentieth century, it had felt the pressures of Russian chauvinism. In novelist Sally Salminen's schoolroom in Vargata, no less than in the schoolrooms of mainland Finland, Russian texts in Swedish translation were used. With the outbreak of hostilities, Russia sought release from the 1856 agreement. The entente powers were not unsympathetic to its attitude, and eventually a Russian garrison of about 6,500 men was established in Åland and limited fortifications were erected. Meanwhile, there was a variety of actions on and reactions to the emerging Åland question. First, Finland endeavoured to make it clear that the islands were a part of the Grand Duchy and not an extension of Russia. Secondly, Sweden set about preparing a case for proclaiming its sovereignty over the islands. Britain and France responded with discussions about the possibility of selling the islands to neutral Sweden, in the same way as Russia had sold Alaska to the USA. Germany reacted with plans for occupying the islands and handing them to Sweden, thereby bringing Sweden into the war on the side of the central powers. One school of thought in Finland, anticipating that war and revolution might offer a road to independence, speculated on the possibility of offering the islands to Sweden in exchange for liberating the Grand Duchy from Russia. *Finland fritt och Åland svenskt* (a free Finland and a Swedish Åland) was the slogan of many Ålanders. In the allied camp, it was held that the status of the islands would raise even greater problems if and when Finland obtained independence. A small group of activists took the initiative in stirring up local sentiment with a view to 'reuniting' Åland with the motherland. Among them, several Ålanders, who had had training with other Finnish *Jägers* in the German army, provided leadership. Julius Sundblom and Alfons Granit were transported by U-boat on special service to Åland and, with a group of friends, provided the inspiration for meetings at Grelsby Kungsgård in Finström, which anticipated an approach being made to Stockholm.

The atmosphere of uncertainty bred growing apprehension among the Ålanders. In December 1917, with Finnish independence recognised by the Russian revolutionary government, but with civil war imminent and Russian troops disaffected throughout Finland, the Ålanders sent a widely supported petition to King Gustaf requesting the 'reunion of the archipelago with Sweden'. To deal with the Russian garrison in Åland, both Finns and Swedes moved in troops. A corps of some 600 'White' Finns crossed the ice to evict the Russians, while Swedish troops arrived from the west to act as mediators and help with their evacuation. A memorial in Godby village recalls some of the skirmishing. But it was clear that a solution to the Åland problem was inseparable from a preliminary solution to the Finnish problem.

The uncertain status of Finland following World War I had its continuing repercussions on Åland. Finns accepted that Russian recognition of independence carried with it recognition of Finland's existing boundaries and, consequently, in Mannerheim's words, that Åland was 'an integral part of Finland'. In the various negotiations to obtain international recognition of Finland, the question of Åland was raised repeatedly. Some argued that, in the light of Finland's economic solvency, it would be wise to sell Åland to Sweden, as Denmark had recently sold the Virgin Islands to the USA. Others suggested territorial exchanges; for example, Finland might receive territorial compensation in Swedish Norrland (where there were a considerable number of Finnish settlers), in Petchenga on the Murmansk coast (to which Finland coveted an Arctic corridor) or in eastern Karelia (where there were Finnish-speaking minorities) in exchange for the Åland archipelago. Russian emigré groups, hopeful that the imperial regime might be restored, argued against the cession of the islands. The British looked for compromises of a constitutional character—there were the examples of the Channel Islands and the Isle of Man. But when, as head of the new Finnish state, Mannerheim visited the king of Sweden in late 1918 and invested him with the Great Cross of the Order of the White Rose, for the first time a ninth rose was incorporated in the chain. It symbolised the ninth province of Finland—Åland.

The problem was lifted to a new level when, following the

armistice of 1918, a deputation of Ålanders went to Paris to plead for independence before the peace conference. Delegates were perplexed and sought to settle the dispute outside the conference. A variety of solutions was proposed, but the Åland problem remained unsolved for more than two years. The general opinion, as summed up by Lord Curzon, was that 'the Finns had the best of the position and the Swedes, on the whole, the best of the argument'. Fundamentally, it was a conflict between ethnography and territoriality. The ethnographic arguments of Sweden were indisputable, but the territorial position of Finland was critical. The issue of Åland's desire for union with Sweden—highly delicate in the postwar climate of national self-determination—had to be balanced against what an American commentator considered the 'cruel and criminal operation' of wrenching the Åland Islands from a politically vulnerable Finland. Versailles negotiators agreed that the matter was outside the jurisdiction of the conference; but, once machinery had been devised for dealing with disputes before the newly created League of Nations, Åland found its rightful court. It was, in fact, the first case to come before the League. The Baltic commission of jurists appointed to look into the problem had not only to detach itself from the emotions that surrounded it, but also to contend with pronouncements which were sometimes made at embarrassingly high levels. It is ironical that within four years of Queen Victoria of Sweden's overtures to Kaiser Wilhelm to help solve the Åland problem, King George V intimated to King Gustaf of Sweden that he was personally in favour of a plebiscite. The press was lively with editorial comment—both independent and sponsored.

The objective of the League of Nations' commission was to seek a solution based on 'common sense and expediency'. With this end in view, some of its members took the initiative of going to see Åland for themselves. The *raison d'être* of the 'natural frontier' between Sweden and Åland was obvious to all who crossed the Åland Sea. Lord Bryce commented feelingly that

Page 107 (*above*) The trawler harbour of Korrvik, just south of Mariehamn;
(*below*) unloading Baltic herring, an important feature of the winter economy

Page 108 (above) The passage
through the winter skerries.
The icebreaker assists
commercial ships;
(left) view of the four-masted
barque *Pommern*, the last ship
of this kind in its authentic
rigging. It belonged to the
Gustav Erikson fleet, but is
now owned by the city of
Mariehamn as a museum

anyone who had travelled by ship from Finland to Sweden would solve the question in a matter of minutes. (In his memoirs, Edvard Westermarck recalled that Bryce's passage had been a rough one.) The only possible alternative boundary to the Åland Sea was Skiftet in the east, described by members of the commission as 'a bad frontier . . . extremely arbitrary from the geographical point of view'. Not surprisingly, out of the minor torrent of papers that was generated, the principle of *Beati possidentes* prevailed, and Finland's sovereignty over the territory was upheld.

At the same time, the agreement concluded by the League of Nations on 27 June 1921 made major concessions to the Ålanders. In the first place, the autonomy law admitted the plea of *Enspråkighet*—the use of Swedish as the primary language. Instruction could only be given in Swedish in schools and Åland would not be required to support schools other than those where Swedish was the language of instruction. Secondly, Ålanders were accorded the right of pre-emption in the purchase of land in their archipelago. Thirdly, they were permitted to use 50 per cent of their land tax revenue for domestic needs. Fourthly, no immigrant was to be accorded a vote in the province until he had fulfilled five years' residence. Fifthly, in choosing a governor for their province, Ålanders were given the right to present a list of candidates to the government in Helsinki. Sixthly, the *Landsting* of Åland had the right to submit through Finland to the Council of the League of Nations any petitions in connection with the guarantees of autonomy contained in the 1921 decision. One observer considered that the guarantees given to the Ålanders amounted to 'the most far-reaching minority rights enjoyed by any group in Europe'.

The solution to the Åland problem was accepted with fair grace by all parties. Sweden's acceptance was most important of all. Perhaps she was already realising that friendship with Finland was more important than the need to have Åland. Anyway, the jurists of the newly fledged League of Nations had done their best. They were sanguine about their judgement. '*Ni fleurs, ni couronnes*', commented the English historian H. A. L. Fisher.

WORLD WAR II

As a sensitive area of a sensitively located state, Åland was automatically implicated in World War II. It was not involved in direct military action, but it was indirectly affected in a variety of ways. During the inter-war years, Åland had remained a quiet part of Europe—a military vacuum. It also lay aside from the mainstream of Finnish political life, though displaying occasional resentment—as, for example, when fennicisation accorded Åland the name Ahvenanmaa in official documents and spread Maarianhamina across the map as the alternative form of Mariehamn. But, by 1938–9, it was evident that Sweden and Finland had to take steps to protect their neutrality. Finland and Sweden agreed that an approach should be made to the League of Nations for permission to erect a limited fortification on the islands. Russian opponents argued publicly that, whatever the fortifications, they might easily be seized and used against the USSR. But privately, proposals—albeit unacceptable to Finland—were circulated. The USSR expressed assent to fortification, if it could take part in their arming and was 'permitted to send an observer to follow the work and subsequently to maintain surveillance over the use of the fortifications'. It was accepted that the activity of the observer would be secret! The establishment of a Russian defence base on the Finnish island of Hogland (F. Suursaari) was the *quid pro quo*. At a later stage, the USSR expressed objection to Sweden sharing in the possible fortification, while Finland was informed by Swedish government circles that any concessions made to Russia in the east—for example, relinquishment of the Karelian isthmus—might lead to Germany counter-balancing by taking Åland. With the outbreak of Fenno-Russian hostilities, on 30 November 1939, Åland found itself caught in the shifting pattern of allegiances that Finland experienced during World War II. On 7 December 1939, the Russians excluded Åland from the blockade that they had imposed on the Finnish coast 'so long as it was not used for military purposes'. Following the Armistice in March 1940, a substantial Russian consulate was established in Mariehamn to keep an eye on possible breaches of the demilitarised status. In April, there were widespread rumours of a German threat of invasion. In 1941, with the outbreak of Finland's Three Year War, Finnish military forces returned to the islands. The few bombs that fell on the islands during the war years were incidental. Åland was most vulnerable at sea; its merchant marine suffered heavily. In the peace settlement of 1944, Åland's status was re-affirmed by the USSR, although there had been rumours that the Russians contemplated the lease of a military base in the archipelago, as an alternative to that which they eventually established in Porkkala to the west of Helsinki.

Åland is no longer discussed in eighteenth-century metaphors. It has ceased to be, as A. F. Skiöldebrand called it, 'the key to Finland'; it is no longer 'a pistol pointed at the breast of Sweden' or, as Valentin Sjöberg likened it, 'Paradise . . . in the shadow of the sword'. It remains at the crossroads of the Baltic, but larger strategies move the giant powers of the present. Internationally, Åland provides a model of a different kind, for its administrative status is of an unusual character. Tore Modeen believes it to have 'the most radical pattern of minority rights' to be found anywhere. As such, it merits attention by international bodies whose ingenuity is taxed by an increasing number of situations in which minority problems call for solutions.

7   LIFE ASHORE

U NTIL the twentieth century, life ashore meant for the
Ålander principally the life of the farmer—or of the
farm labourer. Within three generations there have
been major changes. The first generation responded to the
powerful current of emigration and rejected the homeland.
The second generation witnessed the gradual multiplication of
new forms of employment and opportunity. The third—against
the background of a revolution in personal mobility, the rise of
urbanisation and the integration of Åland into contemporary
Scandinavia's web of systems and organisations—has experienced both a strengthening and a weakening of the security of
life in the islands. The obvious material advantages are offset
partly by psychological disadvantages. In response to these
developments, Ålanders are called upon to make adjustments
and fulfil functions which it is neither physically nor technically
possible to achieve to their satisfaction.

The adjustments are principally in relation to other people
and usually at a personal level. Although they have sailed the
seven seas, Ålanders have coveted the opportunity of being
able to retreat to their home farm or their home island and to
let the world pass by. They have often succeeded in retreating
from the military invasions which have intermittently been the
lot of the islands. But the current experience of invasion—the
tidal wave of summer tourism—is something new. The nature
of the expansion is such that during its annual climax it is
virtually beyond the control of local authorities. The impact
affects all aspects of life and is concentrated most fully on

Mariehamn. Visitors expect it to accommodate and entertain them; natives expect its authorities to preserve and sustain them.

Above and beyond their response to these external forces, Ålanders are called upon to adjust to increasingly fundamental changes in Finnish national policy—policy in relation to the countries of the Nordic Council and policy conditioned by the economic and political decisions of the major European power groups.

THE CHANGING FARM SCENE

To travel through Åland is to be conscious that it is an old-established farming province. To turn the pages of its local newspaper is to learn that, however much the number officially engaged in agriculture has shrunk, Ålanders are near enough to farming both in time and space to have a persistent interest in it. Crop yields are a matter of concern for ordinary people. So, too, are milk yields from the tuberculin-tested and predominantly Ayrshire or Ayrshire-cross cattle. The largest potato or the largest apple of the year can claim a newspaper paragraph in its own right.

Agricultural statistics, kept in a modern form in Åland for five generations, show that the islands constitute a province of owner-operators, though they do not declare how heavy are the mortgages that hang round most farmers' necks. Different agricultural economists provide different answers as to the minimum size of the arable land needed to support a viable holding. Cold statistics indicate that, of Åland's 1,740 farm owners, only twenty-one have more than 30 hectares of cultivated land. The average is 7·66ha per farm. Naturally, quality of soil and intensiveness of production can partly offset restricted farm area. Quality of production and yield per hectare must also be remembered—though the latter is not independent of imported artificial fertilisers. For some crops, such as sugar beet (of which there are 500ha), Åland has the highest yields in the whole of Finland. Sown grasses (occupying 33 per cent of the cultivated area) and grain (occupying 46 per cent) are commonly rotated, with root crops included increasingly. Early potatoes and seed potatoes are especially favoured. The principal farm surpluses exported are wheat (moving directly to the ports of north Finland), sugar beet (going to Nådendal in south-west Finland for refinement), rape seed (to Raisio, near Åbo, for processing), and dairy produce.

The farmer in Åland is at once more favoured and less favoured than the mainland farmer. Åland is the most favoured part of Finland, because the growing season and the grazing season are at their longest. Soils are correspondingly more fertile, added to which they have some of the highest lime contents encountered in Finland. Accordingly, the variety of crops that can be grown takes pride of place for the whole country. Garden crops in Finland proper are translated in status to field crops in Åland. The apple tree thrives; even the plum can be successfully grown. In *The Land of Childhood*, Sally Salminen, the Ålandic writer, recalls red apples in the sunshine as one of her earliest memories; for her, the canopy of branches formed an 'apple heaven'.

On the negative side, extended areas of arable land are limited to parts of the main island. Åland has relatively more impediments in its farmed land than almost any other part of Finland. The intrusive granite bedrock, the broken relief, the scattered boulder fields and the alternation of land and water, hamper farming operations in general and the efficient use of machinery in particular. In Kökar, 3,000 of the 3,300ha of land area are classed as *impedimenter*. In Brändö, the proportion is five-sevenths; in Kumlinge, two-thirds. Such territories are real Jacob's pillows for farmers. Because of the physical fragmentation of the landscape, the average field unit is 1·87ha and the average farm has four of these detached plots. Units are largest in Saltvik (4·27ha) and smallest in Brändö parish (0·79ha).

Enterprise is also increasingly inhibited by the limited provincial market and the cost of transport to mainland markets.

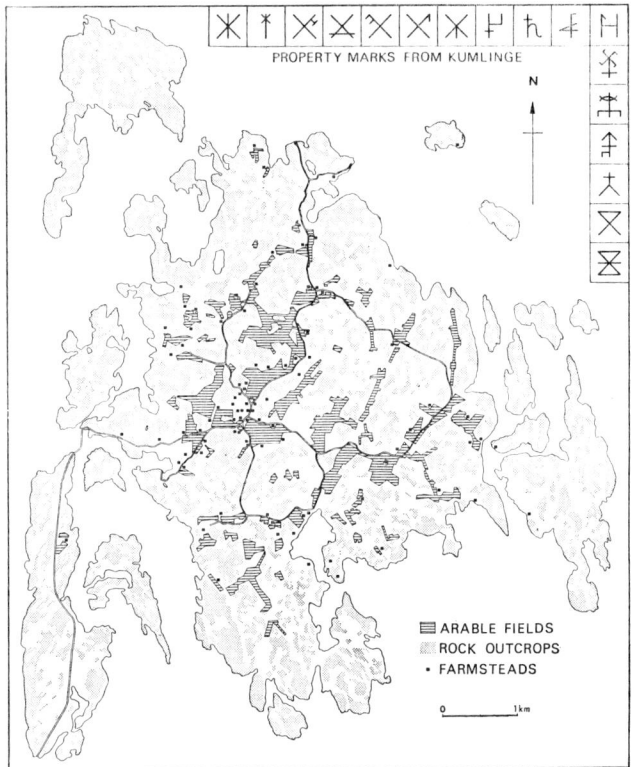

PROPERTY MARKS FROM KUMLINGE

N

ARABLE FIELDS
ROCK OUTCROPS
• FARMSTEADS

0   1km

Contemporary land use on the main island of Kumlinge parish

Farming difficulties are exaggerated because increasingly efficient farming in both Sweden and Finland has led to over-production of certain products which are Ålandic staples. Furthermore, in an economy where farming has been built up and sustained by a structure of subsidies, Åland's farmers have come to rely upon a system of supports which are now being eroded at the national level. The Åland archipelago, as with most Finnish island groups, enjoys agricultural supports of a more generous character than those accorded to all of Finland except the north-east. But, in the final instance, it is not economic to export farm products from Finland, so that domestic output must be brought into line with domestic demand. The decline of dairy cattle (from 8,000 to 5,700 in the decade 1960–70) and the retreat of farming from the periphery of Åland to its core, are thus partly explained in terms of national policies. Again, though climatic conditions are favourable, they are only favourable when Åland is compared with other high latitude areas. The risks of drought during the growing season are a particular distraction. Field operations are rigorously controlled by the swing of the seasons and there are corresponding rhythms of seasonal unemployment and over-employment in the countryside. Admittedly, Ålanders are predominantly mixed farmers and since livestock is stall-fed for about seven months, they are not without some regular winter labour. In addition, some farmers will transfer their energies from farming to forestry when snow covers the ground.

For the line of the forest is everywhere on the horizon, as it is on the Finnish mainland, so that the farmer is reminded of the origin of his farmland. However, although Åland has some of Finland's most favoured circumstances for plant growth, it has only limited areas of good softwood forests. And, partly because of the fragmented character of forest ownership, Ålanders have pushed forward with less vigour the rationalisation of forest operations and woodland improvement than has been the case in Finland proper. Yearly production of timber is a modest 180,000cu m. Production is inadequate to meet the needs of a modern mill in Åland; though the woodchip mill at Godby, exporting direct to Sweden, indicates a new trend. Saw mills produce about 150,000cu m of timber annually. Farm timber is still widely cut for fencing, fuel and other domestic uses. Nor have domestic animals ceased to use the woodlands for grazing; while the tufted crowns of deciduous trees recall the recency of pollarding for sheep fodder.

The reaction of the Ålandic farmer to present-day opportunities is threefold. First, he aims to increase to the full the variety of his activities—or, to put it another way, to spread as widely as possible the risks to which he is exposed. Secondly, he pushes as hard as possible to have the risks cushioned by government protection of one sort or another; this in the face of diminishing sympathy at the national level for the farm lobby. Thirdly, he underwrites farm enterprise with profits from the sea—a centuries-old tradition expressed above all in the disproportionately large and expensive farm buildings that everywhere dominate the landscape. All of these reactions indicate that the farm scene in Åland is less easily explained than a superficial glance would suggest.

DIVERSIFICATION OF ENTERPRISE

Diversity of production is the most obvious characteristic. Åland never had a more varied agriculture nor a larger output in relation to its farmed area than today. While Åland's farming has always displayed a combination of activities, the combinations have changed and specialisation has acquired a new importance. Within the traditional framework of field husbandry, Åland has developed specialisations. Some 160–180ha of onions—rejoicing in the varietal names Excellent, Enormous, Sublima—are planted annually. Gherkins are cultivated by the hectare and exported by the boatload to the mainland market. So are carrots, beetroot and cabbages (the last in response to an expanding demand which, it is estimated, could increase tenfold), and the inevitable dill and parsley. Vårdö has nearly half of Åland's fruit acreage. Its 2,000 apple trees are now supplemented by small fruit crops, such as black currants and strawberries grown under contract. There is also increasing specialisation in greenhouse crops, though Åland has no particular advantage over the mainland in this respect. The first commercial greenhouses were built in 1947; today there are 20,000sq m under glass and the largest commercial greenhouse covers 1,000sq m. Tomatoes are the chief crop under glass; but lettuce and other salad crops are also grown. Chrysanthemums and carnations are the principal cut flowers —in a part of the world where flowers play an important part in social etiquette. Save in the summer, one of the problems is the provision of heated transport to market. Cold greenhouses and plastic shelters are invaluable for hurrying on early crops of cauliflowers, salad vegetables and strawberries for the tourist trade. Outlying Brändö has proportionately the largest area under glass, partly because it has more adequate supplies of soft water. All field husbandry and horticultural crops are the direct concern of Jomala agricultural research station, the officials of which keep a watchful eye on the best seed strains to distribute.

Another specialist pursuit, and one which is an established prerogative of Finland's coasts and archipelagos, is fur farming. Production from two dozen farms is about 20,000 skins a year. Åland's largest mink farm has more than 3,000 animals producing about 2,000 skins a year (and a related problem of disposing of the carcasses). The average stock of mink per farm is 200–300, relatively small scale by comparison with enterprises on the Finnish mainland. It is a sensitive trade, the whim of fashion affecting the value of different colours, let alone that of mink themselves. A farm advertised for sale in 1972 comprised 'eight houses with accommodation for 2,000 mink, including 578 females and 98 males of standard colour, sapphire, pearl, topaz and black cross'. Fox farming, out of fashion for a generation, is slowly returning.

Side by side with diversification runs the need for an ever-widening range of mechanical equipment and a corresponding need for the multiplication of technical skills. The milking machine, modest in cost, is almost ubiquitous. The extent of the cultivated area theoretically restricts the economic use of many machines on most farms, but prestige frequently outweighs economy. Investment of capital per hectare is consequently high; so, too, are costs of maintenance. The tractor, with its various attachments, has become increasingly economic because it has been scaled down in size and cost to meet the purses of smallholders. It has driven out the horse, of which not more than 200 remain. The combine harvester, even though modelled to meet the needs of smallholdings, is not an economic piece of equipment for many of the farms on which it is employed. Potato and sugar beet harvesters are also warranted on only relatively few farms. Such equipment appears side by side in a countryside where the hewing of wood, the drawing of water and even foraging for winter fodder may still be practised with almost biblical simplicity. And, although the telephone and electricity serve almost all farms, piped water is unusual and the earth closet commonplace.

In a variety of ways, cooperative organisations help the situation. Beside milk collection and processing, marketing of foodstuffs, bulk purchase of raw materials and equipment, the farmers' cooperative societies have done much to improve the quality of livestock. On most Åland farms, the dairy herd averages less than ten and it is uneconomic to keep a bull, let alone one of high quality. Cooperatively-owned thoroughbred bulls, coupled with artificial insemination, have helped to change the quality of the dairy herd. Cooperative experience has also helped with the introduction of large-scale machines, such as fodder pelletisation machines or ditch-digging and clearing machines—a fundamental aid in farmland which is drained principally by open ditches.

Cooperation, intensification, mechanisation and diversification accompany a distribution of production which is more limited today than for many generations. The frontiers of farming, pushed to their absolute limits in the nineteenth century, have been steadily retreating for two generations. The retreat has been the consequence of both attraction and propulsion. The attractions of more remunerative employment have drawn younger people away from the farms. The farm population is an ageing population. Ålandic specialities such as mink farming and greenhouse cultivation are labour intensive, so that their costs of production will inevitably rise. The retreat of the arable frontier has been complemented by the advance of the waste or by reafforestation. In its own right and providing labour is available, the harvest from the wasteland is not negligible. The cowberry is an export product; blueberries, mushrooms and hazel nuts provide valued local harvests, and the rosehip is picked as a health food.

It is evident that farming has gone through a great deal of change in a very short time. Land abandonment has succeeded to land reclamation; land improvement is more significant than the search for new land. It is difficult to realise that in the 1950s Ålanders were being chided for their lack of enterprise in not expanding their cultivated area. Theoretically, Åland lends itself to coastal reclamation and at least one major imaginative project has been conceived. Lumparen is an extensive shallow embayment which, by comparison with reclamation along the tidewater lands of the North Sea, could be easily diked and yield thousands of acres of new land. Today, with the demand for most Åland farm products stationary, or in retreat, the time for investment in such a project is not propitious.

It is the source of money for investment at lowlier levels which is the more lively concern of the rural community. Cheap loans for the installation of water supply and electricity, for the construction of farm buildings and land drainage—let alone for pension schemes—are the central topics of discussion in farming circles. To use Léouzon le Duc's phrase from over a century ago, when these topics are invoked, the Åland farmer's 'taciturnity gives way to prodigious loquacity'.

THE HOMESTEAD

According to farm statistics, the average farmer is over fifty years old. *Ålands Bebyggelse*, a book containing pictures of most of Åland's homesteads, suggests that the majority of farmers occupy spacious clapboard homes, warm beneath pine shingles, locally made tiles or painted zinc sheeting. Houses and farm buildings are usually located on rocky outcrops. Mostly, they are painted a warm copper red; sometimes a deep ochre is favoured. The earlier scatter of farm buildings has been generally reduced to an all-purpose unitary structure, though some hundreds of them are in need of renovation or modernisation. On the ground floor are housed the animals—all are indoors for at least six months of the year—together with dairy facilities, garage and tractor shed. The upper storey, approached by a ramp, accommodates fodder, machinery, equipment and the increasingly neglected sledges. A silo tower of cement blocks is incorporated in the building. The whole complex is commonly fenced around with post and rail; the old slatted fences still survive, as well as the stone walls that are testimony to generations of boulder clearance from the arable land. Barbed wire is the most common fencing material, together with electric fences for controlled grazing.

Maturity is given to most farmhouses by the established groves or avenues of birch, rowan or maple. The garden grows out of the rocky waste, woodland or farmed land. Cultivated and wild plants merge, especially in the outer islands. Only rarely is there a dividing hedge of Siberian pea. Apple trees, lilac, viburnum and roses rise above the gooseberries, currants, raspberries and rhubarb that thrive beside an abundance of flowers and vegetables which, leaping to ripeness in the warm, thundery weather, convey momentary illusions of the deep south. The tough *Rosa rugosa*, bright dahlias, marigolds, petunias, yellow Rudbeckias, mountain ash, crimson maple, and the trailing red Virginia creeper, give richer autumn colourings than in most parts of Finland.

Indoors, the inter-communicating rooms contain a blend of old and new. Painted wooden furniture, painted floors (often partly covered by striped handmade rag rugs), shining 2·5m high tile-stoves, rocking chair, loom and grandfather clock balance electric cooker, refrigerator, washing machine and television (with both Swedish and Finnish transmissions). Piped water is customary on the main island, though the well is still common. Windows (double-glazed in winter) contain the usual Scandinavian jungle of flowering plants, the larger of which may include such exotic species as plumbago, amaryllis, bougainvillea and stephanotis. The *bastu* (which is Swedish for *sauna*), an established feature in Åland, seems to have spread in from the Finnish mainland in the nineteenth century.

THE RISE OF THE WORKSHOP INDUSTRY

Agriculturally based industries are small scale and often continue old traditions. Milling is one of the oldest. The picturesque wooden windmills, restored with such loving care, recall an ancient industry which is now pursued in cooperatively owned milling plants. The first cooperative dairy was started in 1893, since when dairy production has been concentrated in Mariehamn, with ferry and lorry collecting milk daily. Butter and cheese surplus to Åland's needs move to mainland Finland. Mariehamn's slaughtery, which has a capacity to deal with 1 million kg of meat a year, also serves the needs of the entire archipelago. One of the most profitable Åland enterprises is the production of chipped potatoes for export. By comparison with these all-year-round activities, fish processing (eg filleting in Föglö and Brändö) has seasonal peaks and troughs, while fruit conservation and cucumber pickling are late-summer pursuits. There is also limited brick and tile production (in Hammarland), manufacture of small-scale cement products, and sand and gravel working for highway and construction activities.

Most workshop industry is concentrated in and around Mariehamn. There are natural economies in concentration— not least of labour supply. Workshop industries look to local skills: saw-milling, furniture and cabinet making, boat building and repairing, engineering and maintenance, clothing, textiles and shoe-making. There are small-scale assembly industries and, inevitably, exceptions to the general pattern, eg stove manufacture. The local market is too small for the development of metallurgical industry, except for repairs. Indeed, although new enterprises receive tax relief for the first five to ten years, by comparison with mainland Finland workshop industry is at a disadvantage. Åland has an absolute deficiency of indigenous energy supplies. Imported oil costs about twice as much as in Nyland (Uusimaa) province and, since oil is the basis for Åland's thermo-electric plant, so too does electricity. Although there is a 170km electric cable from Väddö in Sweden to Tellholm in Hammarland, this is likely to do little to ease costs. While labour tends to be cheaper in Åland, as soon as it has tasted the pleasures of urban Mariehamn and acquired adequate skills, it tends to migrate to Sweden. Swedish factories advertise regularly for labour in Åland. It will be apparent that outside Mariehamn there are only very restricted employment opportunities for women. This is undoubtedly a fact which explains the higher migration rate of female labour.

From time to time, larger scale industry is contemplated. In the 1950s, there was heavy investment in the underwater Nyhamn iron ore mine. The lofty ventilation shaft and its 250m lift remain, but the mine has never been operational. Again, using submerged Palaeozoic limestones akin to those on the mainland, it would be possible to establish a cement industry. By and large, however, Åland is not a favourable industry area. Its maritime enterprise is the counterpart to industry on the mainland.

THE NETWORK OF COMMUNICATIONS

Historically, Åland has looked to the post road—the arterial route linking the east and west ferry points. Contemporarily, its road system traces an entirely different pattern. The change took place when Mariehamn became a trading centre in its own right and when direct shipping connections between Sweden and Finland replaced the old post route. All roads now lead to—or from—Mariehamn, and the traffic-flow diagram below emphasises this fact. At the same time, the development of the communicational network looks to the strengthening of through routes rather than the multiplication of dead-end trails.

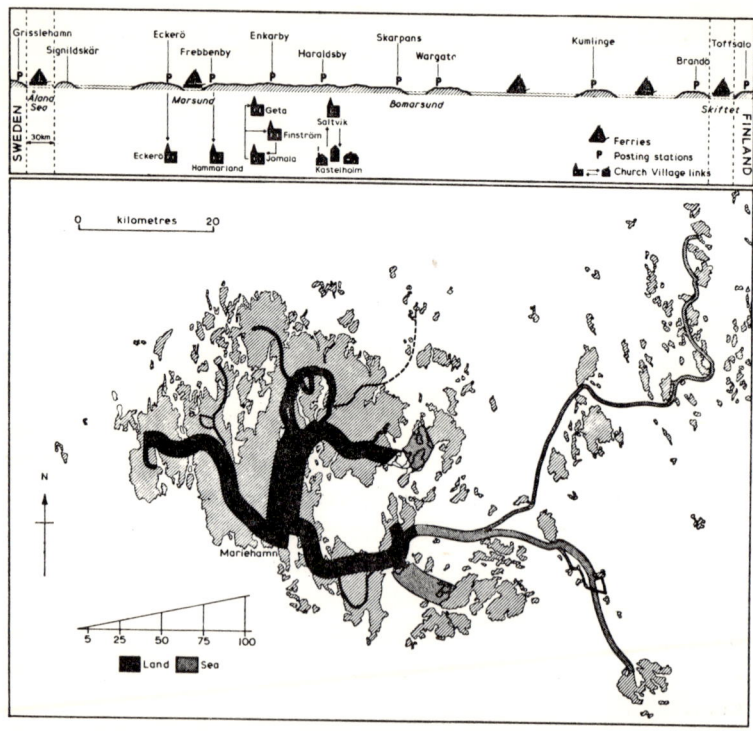

(*top*) The historic post route from Sweden to Finland; (*bottom*) motor-bus and ferry communications, 1973

Åland's roads serve the needs of the 5,844 (1970) cars registered in the islands, and many times that number brought in aboard the ferries during the height of the holiday season.

Page 125   A winter car ferry

Page 126 (above) The *Skärgårdsfarjan*, a small car ferry that runs between the main archipelago islands and the mainland; (below) the west harbour of Marie-hamn with a ferryboat from Sweden alongside the quay. The swift development of the tourist trade has made large harbour installations necessary, although they are not shown in the picture

Daily bus services ply from all corners of the main island, performing the general delivery service of the old-time carriers, transporting mail, packages and newspapers as well as passengers. They tie in with ferries to Vårdö, Kumlinge, Brändö, Kökar, Sottunga and Föglö (which has its own limited bus system). Cars also use the limited stretches of road on these same outlying islands. On smaller islands, the tractor serves the purpose of a car. The bicycle is still actively employed in Åland, for pleasure as well as for the sport that reaches its climax in the annual race round the main island.

Only about a quarter of Åland's 800km of roads are surfaced, and cheap asphalt (a by-product of Finnish oil refining) has only appeared during the last decade. The road system is extremely sensitive to the morphology of the land and the shapes of property boundaries. There is a constant cry for better roads, for more roads and more bridges, though in recent years a number of time-consuming ferries between the mainland parishes have been replaced by bridges. Because most of the costs of construction and maintenance of communications fall on the very restricted Åland exchequer, and because there is an infinity of competing claims for assistance, road improvements are necessarily limited. As everywhere in these latitudes, climate takes its toll of road surfaces. Snow clearance is only a problem in exceptional years, but frost upheaval in spring interferes with extensive stretches of road.

The establishment of an ice cover opens up the possibility of winter roads. Ferry routes may be replaced by ice roads; short cuts are made across embayments. An ice road is opened to Åbo in hard winters, with as many as 100 cars a day risking its surface for several weeks on end. In 1970, an ice road 110km in length was operated between Sund and Gustavs (Kustavi) on the Finnish mainland. Motorists are warned that they drive at their own risk over such highways and it is not unknown for them to disappear through the ice. In winter, roads are frequented by the century-old *sparkstötting*, the snow scooter, a cheap and practical conveyance on which it is possible to cover tens of kilometres at considerable speed. The motorised snow scooter—the North American skidoo—reverberates increasingly in the winter archipelago, while the ski has come back into its own in a big way.

When summer takes over, the cross-country ski track becomes the footpath. Åland is attractive walking country, with plenty of local variations in contour, rock formations and vegetation. The possibility of escaping from the beaten track increases as long-forgotten footpaths are brought back into being. They reach their climax in the high country of the north. From Hultaberget in Sund, Orrdalsklint and Kasberg in Saltvik, to Getaberg in Geta, there are marked routes which command broad vistas over the fiorded north coast as well as down the gentle dip-slope to the south. They incorporate traverses across the boulder-strewn raised beaches and offer side tracks to high level caverns, such as Kloddstugan.

Åland began to look to the air in the 1920s. It was natural that its first aircraft should be seaplanes; water surfaces were available for landing, but extended flat surfaces of well-drained land were very limited. Not until 1940 was a landing ground established in the vicinity of Mariehamn; it trespassed upon farmland and called for large-scale drainage schemes. It has become Åland's modest airport and is linked several times a day to international airports in Stockholm and Åbo. No other landing ground exists, though facilities for Kumlinge are debated. Medical and veterinary services, emergency supplies and assistance are provided by helicopter or light amphibious planes. From outlying parts of the archipelago, children are ferried to school on Sunday night or Monday morning and home again on Friday evening.

Other forms of communication are even livelier. The printed word circulates with a minimum of time and, as befits a Scandinavian town, Mariehamn has excellent bookshops. It is nearly a century since the first manuscript news sheet, *Marie-*

hamnsbladet, began its brief life (1878–80). In 1891, the news-paper *Åland* was born; it is printed three times weekly. The most widely circulated national newspapers in Åland are Helsinki's *Hufvudstadsbladet* and Stockholm's *Dagens Nyheten* and *Expressen.* A local radio service operates and a television transmission centre was established in 1970; but it is the telephone that really binds Åland together, with vital lines sometimes looped in the most casual way through woodlands and across intervening waters. Almost every Åland home is on the telephone, the directory listing 8,000 subscribers. The system dates from 1887, though telegraph links existed earlier. In 1876, a line was constructed from Åland to the Finnish mainland at Nystad (Uusikaupunki) and the following year the *Store Nordisk Telegrafselskab* constructed a cable from the main island to Grisslehamn in Sweden. The telephone service, which is operated jointly with the postal service, is state-owned.

POPULATION MIGRATION

Åland has always known a fair amount of population mobility. During the last 100 years it has reached its highest proportions; during the last generation, its maximum. Migration and emigration are inseparable. A century ago, Åland had a remark-ably even distribution of population; today, the distribution is increasingly uneven. In some respects, the drift from the land and the modest urbanisation represented by Mariehamn are positive developments. Parts of rural Åland were overpopulated at the turn of the century, while a concentration of population in one centre helps with provincial organisation. The peak develop-ment of Mariehamn occurred in the decade 1950–60, during which its population increased by 3,415—or more than 100 per cent. On the other hand, the provision of services at large in areas not only thinly peopled but in which population is unevenly scattered and fast declining causes administrative headaches.

Furthermore, as a province of Finland—albeit of autonomous status—Åland has to be set in its national context. Population mobility, with its associated changes in the structure of population independently of its distribution, is a matter of degree. There are other parts of Finland where the intensity of migration and its consequences are as great if not greater than in Åland. There are other parts of Finland where population is as thin if not thinner upon the ground than in Åland—and where physical circumstances are worse. A statistically minded country has aimed at measuring these problems and has aspired to produce quantitative solutions. In the formulae that are produced to express the degree of disadvantage, Åland has its appointed places. The Finnish government identifies two different development areas; Åland belongs to the second category. The levels of financial assistance, financial relief, subsidies and price adjustments are arranged accordingly.

Intensity of migration from place to place is a response to a multitude of different factors. These also change in time. Among the propulsive forces has been over-population. By the end of the nineteenth century, much of Åland's countryside carried too many people. Some of the peripheral areas, where new fisher-farmsteads had been created, were adequate to support a single family, but inadequate as the family multiplied. Fragmentation of marginal holdings on the death of the owner led to increasing hardship, a reduction of living standards and to migration to presumed more favoured opportunities. The sea had always provided a measure of relief to pressure on the land, but the sea was not enough. Emigration was a safety valve, but emigration was an extreme remedy. Migration inside Åland only made sense as opportunities other than farming were created and as provision for training became available.

Migration can be traced from the summary tables of annual registration (*mantalslängd*) which are maintained in each parish by the representative of the Ministry of the Interior. The tables indicate date and place of birth of residents, in-migration and out-migration. In earlier times, the church registers provided a record of movement in and out of the parish. Between 1950 and 1970, the population of the province of Åland fell slightly (from 21,700 to 20,400); that of Mariehamn more than doubled (from 4,600 to 8,400); that of rural Åland fell sharply (from 17,000 to 12,000).

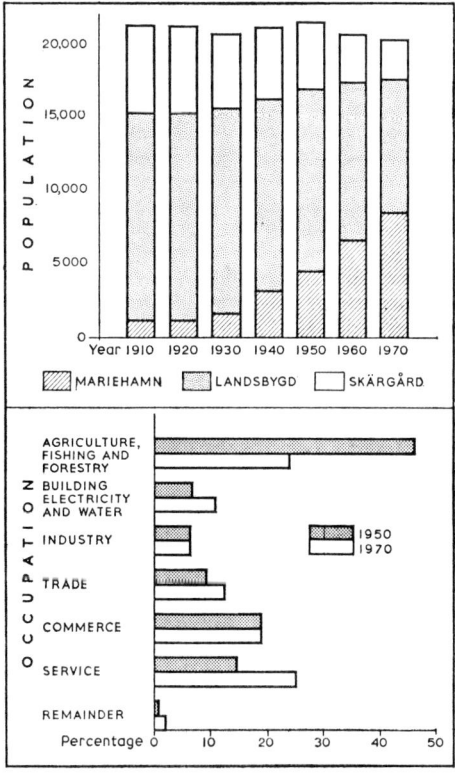

The changing distribution of population and employment

There have been a number of contrasting consequences. First of all, the local population structures have been widely affected. Age structure is normally represented by bar dia-

131

grams and in a stable community the model assumes a pyramidal form. The diagram of population pyramids illustrates the relatively stable situation for the Åland Islands in 1750. The rest of the bar diagrams are for 1970. Mariehamn displays an exceptional age structure. In the rural parishes the younger age groups are numerically small by comparison with the old age groups, a fact which might be explained by a decline in the birth rate, by out-migration (particularly of families with children and of women of child-bearing age), or by a combination of both. One interesting point is that, despite migration, there is little visual testimony of overall population contraction.

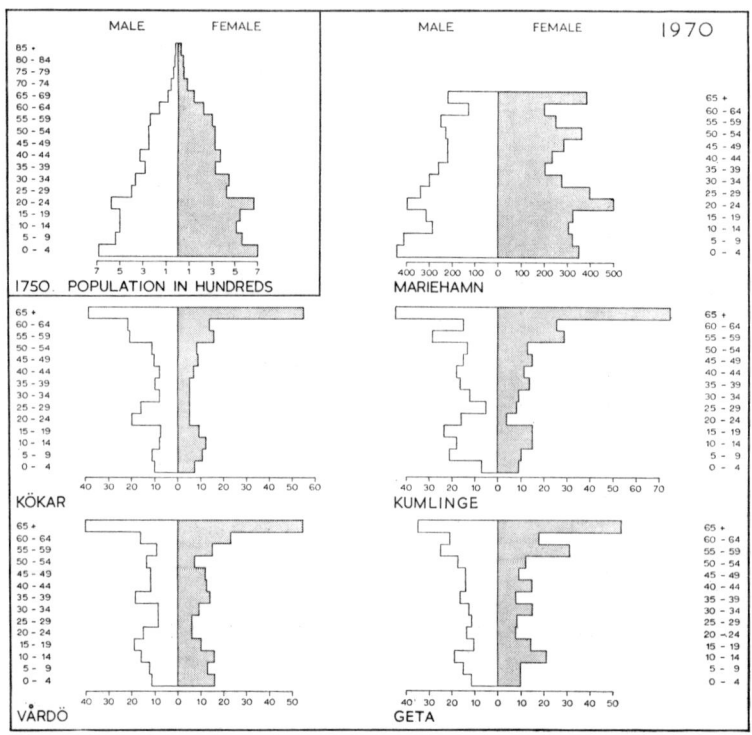

Population pyramids for sample parishes, 1970, with a pyramid for 1750

Improved living standards and investment in machinery have resulted in standards of cultivation and maintenance which are an improvement over those of former times. And, as indicated below, the acquisition of the remoter abandoned farms by summer vacationists has restored them in most cases to at least their earlier estate. There are arguments both for and against regarding the drift to the town and beyond as less of a retrogressive tendency than a rationalisation of a difficult rural situation.

Migration is inseparable from emigration. Indeed, outmigration from the parent parish is frequently the first step towards movement beyond provincial and national frontiers. Emigration has not had a consistent character; during the middle and later nineteenth century, there was a regular migration to the towns of the Finnish mainland and often from there to St Petersburg. The tide of emigration that flowed to the New World from Sweden and Finland also carried Ålanders with it. They moved especially to the USA, where many of their descendants still maintain links with the homeland and support their own Åland Society. They were strengthened by smaller-scale movements after the two world wars, when a part of the stream was also diverted to Australia. Edvard Westermarck, the social anthropologist, who was familiar with Åland from his younger days, considered that emigration sprang from the absence of a sense of obligation to the homeland. But many Ålanders had little reason to be emotionally attached to the land; most had insufficient land to meet their needs; many had insufficiently rewarding land; some had none at all. As with other Scandinavians who suffered this deprivation, the image of the land of the free shone bright with the promise of free land. Some migrated from Åland for political reasons. Russian chauvinism was felt in Åland as elsewhere in Finland and, when Finland itself became independent, there was fear of Finnish chauvinism. Following the refusal of the League of Nations to permit the unification of Åland with Sweden, there was a certain amount of emigration to Sweden. As Åland has settled more securely into its politically autonomous frame, the image of Sweden has begun to change. More Ålanders migrate to Sweden than ever, though not for the same reasons; and they are more sanguine in their attitudes. The belief that material conditions are better in Sweden is widespread, but there are fewer illusions that Sweden is a better country in which to live. The existence of a common Nordic labour market is slowly smoothing out the differentials.

The steady migration to the Finnish mainland is complemented by immigration from mainland Finland to Åland, especially to Mariehamn. Indeed, about a quarter of the population of Mariehamn was born on the mainland, and only one third in the town itself.

During the 1960s, the rate of emigration from Åland averaged 400 a year. Emigrants were young rather than middle-aged or old, and female rather than male. Although there were about 200 immigrants annually, mostly from other parts of Finland, the population no longer maintained itself. The extremity of the impact was felt in the most inaccessible parts, with desertion of settlements into which people pressed with such colonial vigour a century ago. Between 1905 and 1960, no fewer than sixty of Åland's inhabited islands were deserted. The consequences of emigration have tended to be exaggerated by a falling birth rate; though Åland has an unexpected bonus in that it has the highest twinning rate for any part of Europe. By comparison with Finland at large, the percentage of the population over fifty years of age is higher, while the percentages of population under twenty, of men between twenty and thirty and of women between twenty and twenty-five are all lower than the national average. Emigration and immigration appear to be increasingly sensitive processes for Åland. They are inseparable from the behaviour of the Swedish labour market and the largely independent upswings and downswings of the Ålandic economy. Forecasting population movements is an unusually hazardous pursuit about which Åland's planners are increasingly cautious. Furthermore, migratory movements at large have cumulative consequences for different parts of Finland. Thus, population decline is accompanied by a decline in local tax returns and may be accompanied by a reduction in local subsidies.

THE PROVISION OF SERVICES

In the context of migration, of emigration, of the dwindling rural population and of the annual tidal wave of tourists, the provision of necessary services is a growing problem. So far as the rural communities are concerned, it is all right as long as they have tolerable access to Mariehamn. But, even then, there are certain services which must be provided locally. The problem is relatively common in Scandinavia and statistical investigations into the minimum viable population required to support different types of service have been conducted. The minimum satisfactory level for a parish centre to support a school, cooperative store, bank, post office, old people's home, district nurse, etc, is about 3,000. Outside Mariehamn, no commune in Åland approaches this number of inhabitants. The largest are Jomala (c 2,000) and Finström (c 1,700). Moreover, the number of social services demanded increases, the minimum viable population rises steadily (a growth rate of 4 per cent annually is estimated for Sweden), the actual population remains stationary where it does not decline, and the average age of the inhabitants rises. The ageing process in Åland's rural communities raises problems in its own right.

There are two main solutions. The first is to concentrate the services and to bring the consumer to them. For this reason, the concentration of many activities in Mariehamn represents one form of rationalisation. But it still leaves the greater part of the archipelago with the problem that medical, dental, ophthalmic and pharmaceutical services are needed most badly by the

135

elderly or the very young—those least physically able to make the necessary journey. The second and complementary solution is to provide regular mobile services. Mobile shops and libraries, afloat as well as awheel, provide examples. Vicars with extensive inland parishes make their seasonal perambulations, holding services in private homes. Medical, agricultural and fishery consultation is also provided by officers who move around the countryside.

Problems of marketing and supply are eased by farmers' and fishermen's cooperative organisations. As with other Baltic archipelagos, Åland is especially sensitive to milk collection; the presence or absence of a milk boat is frequently critical for the continuation or abandonment of a farmstead. Speedy and regular transport for fresh fish and vegetables is equally necessary. The provision of all of these services is expensive and, in general, uneconomic. On the other hand, it is socially desirable. Nothing can contribute more to the stability and individuality of Åland than concern for the individual Ålander. Of course, compromises are required. 'The clock does not matter here,' declared a Kumlinge resident, 'except twice a day when the ferry comes.' It is a big car ferry which must combat winter ice to bring all the necessary goods and to carry as many islanders as wish to travel with their free passes.

To the general problems of servicing must be added those that are particular to tourism. In the first place, Åland lacks a full and balanced range of skilled labour. The implications are immediately felt in the building boom consequent upon immigration to Mariehamn and the rise of the holiday industry. While Mariehamn's acute housing shortage is a phenomenon common to most of Finland's expanding towns, solutions are the more difficult because of the competition for limited labour supplies between house building and hotel construction. Contract labour from Sweden and Finland arranged by construction companies is short-term and is not geared to longer-term maintenance needs. Water supply and waste disposal become critical areas of concern in this context. As a seasonal activity, tourism also calls for a summer army of skilled service personnel. For approximately three months, the ferries need 600 additional crew; the management side of hotels, banks, garages and shops calls for an extra 500 skilled staff, while about 1,000 semi-skilled assistants are required. Retail trading is under particular pressure. There must be stock-piling (and risk-taking) to meet the shopping demands of the daily invasion of Stockholmers. The meat trade is especially sensitive. The size of the tourist demand for foodstuffs and general goods is such that the bulk of their material needs must be imported to Åland.

It is upon Mariehamn that all this impinges. Mariehamn was never an epitome of Åland. Tourism, a one-time luxury trade which has become a folk movement, has thrust it into an even more anomalous position. The concentrated multitudes that are transforming Mariehamn are largely urban residents with urban attitudes. They compete for the attention of its limited cadre of administrators at a time when the demand for an understanding of rural Åland is increasingly insistent. Mariehamn has been accustomed to dealing with the rural needs of countryfolk and its services have been traditionally geared to the requirements of scattered settlements. It is all too easy to subordinate the needs of individual farmers and fisherfolk to the collective demands of the summer invasion. In this problem, Åland faces a dilemma common to island communities in many parts of the world.

8   LIFE AFLOAT

ÅLAND is wedded to the sea. For most of the year the archipelago is tied together by shipping; at the same time much of its wealth derives from trading on the high seas. To their traditional experience in sea-going, Ålanders have added expertise in navigation. In Mariehamn, the contents of the nautical museum illustrate how Åland's shipping has arrived at its present estate, while the navigation school—a century old in 1967, supporting a radar device in its roof-top crow's nest and appropriately situated in Neptune Street—guarantees that crews shall keep abreast of the modern disciplines that complement the historic arts of seamanship. The same radio and electronic devices that help to maintain the clockwork efficiency of the ferry services keep shipping companies (*skeppsrederier*, as they are called in the vernacular) in continuous contact with a world-wide fleet, the daily movements of which are reported in the press as a matter of direct concern to ordinary Ålanders. It is said that the first question on the lips of every waking Ålander used to be 'which way is the wind blowing today?' The elements still stir the majority of the people, who are bred with a healthy respect for the behaviour of the sea. They enjoy its restlessness and adapt to its moods partly because, at an early age, they are taught never to play with it.

Ships have a protean quality; they change form, they multiply. Åland has both suffered and benefited from the increasing specialisation of shipping at a world level and from the unparalleled volume and variety of vessels that operate locally.

Five principal types of ship use its territorial waters. Largest are the commercial ferries that ply between the main island and Sweden (Stockholm, Norrtälje, Kapellskär and Grisslehamn) and the Finnish mainland (Åbo and Nådendal). They are complemented by the subsidised domestic ferry routes between the main islands, especially the links to the north-east, from Långnäs, via Kumlinge and Brändö to the coast of Gustavs; to Sottunga and Kökar; to Vårdö. Secondly, there are modest cargo vessels—the larger cargo ships registered in Mariehamn rarely if ever return to their home port. Cargo ships range from the fast disappearing wooden yawls to the small oil tankers that meet Åland's domestic needs. Thirdly, there is the fishing fleet —the trawlers, all of a kind and distinguishable from the rest of Finland's trawling fleet only by their numbers, and the smaller, often open-decked, boats owned by the fisher-farmers. Fourthly, there are pleasure craft. Although the outboard motor is everywhere, sail still propels a substantial fleet of yachts. Finally, there are the grey, high-powered coastguard cutters, indispensable providers of emergency services rather than interceptors on behalf of the law.

Most shipping disappears from Ålandic waters during winter; much of it is laid up until the disappearance of the ice. As a result, *vinterliggare*—as these ships have been known through the centuries—remain a feature of the islands. Around Mariehamn, a growing shortage of summer moorings is followed by a premium on space for hauling up in winter. The ferries continue inexorably. They rarely need the assistance of icebreakers, but are straitjacketed in channels kept open through the ice. Where pilots are needed (or demanded by union regulations) they may drive to the ship's side by tractor or jeep. Coastguard officials exchange their cutters for the skidoo that speeds them over the frozen inshore waters.

KNOWLEDGE OF THE WATERS

Intensification of life afloat has called for increasing knowledge of the coasts and understanding of the offshore waters. The charting of Åland's waters was pressed forward by the Swedish naval authorities in the last two decades of the eighteenth century. Under the direction of Nathaniel af Schultén, with the patient use of plumb-line from row-boats in summer and through ice holes from horse-drawn sleighs in winter, the first detailed reconnaissance of Åland's territorial waters was made. Many of the flimsy working papers that bear testimony to the meticulous labours of the survey crews are in the library of Åbo Akademi. Not until the inter-war years were adequate navigational charts of Åland available for general use; final correction of them was speeded up by the introduction of the echo sounder. The territorial waters of the archipelago are charted on a scale 1 : 50,000. The charts—contoured at 3, 6, 10, 20 and 40m, with additional soundings and with magnetic anomalies and marked channels recorded—are indispensable to the flotillas of vessels, national and international, that crowd the territorial waters of Åland.

The seamarks that have multiplied simultaneously were for a long time less than the complex waterways warranted. But beacons and lights cost money. A system of lighthouses was constructed from the 1820s onwards. In the lamps that were introduced to them, hemp oil gave way to American petroleum in the 1870s and to Russian petroleum twenty years later. Lonely rocks, such as Sälskär, were marked by them. And the greater the hazard, the more impressive the warning. So impressive was Bogskär lighthouse, built in 1880, that it had to be destroyed for security reasons in World War I; reconstructed, it suffered the same fate in World War II. There are also lightships such as that at Sydbrotten. Automation has greatly eased their manning.

In addition to these major features, there is a constellation of fixed beacons that flash, blink and beam in green, red and white by night. Hierarchically beneath them is a bizarre miscellany of light buoys, spar buoys, bell buoys and wooden seamarks, that range from the formal to the seemingly informal birch-twig 'broomsticks'. The coming of radar has greatly facilitated the passage of Åland's tortuous fairways. The fall in cost of echo-sounding devices has brought them within the purses of even small-scale fishermen.

In winter, the islands share in the elaborate system of ice-reporting that has been developed in Sweden and Finland during the last seventy years. Daily charts of the distribution and character of sea ice are issued from Stockholm and Helsinki, while forecasts are made of the likely advance, retreat or general development of ice around Åland as a component in the Central Baltic system. All this is a far cry from the system of cannon shots initiated from the island of Signildskär off Eckerö in 1789 to indicate to travellers on the Swedish coast the nature of intervening ice conditions. The use of the cannon was replaced in 1796 by an optical telescope constructed according to the principle of the French inventor, Claude Chappe. With the aid of a large frame, into which a series of panels could be slotted, a code book and clear weather, it was possible to dispatch information on ice conditions and, indeed, hundreds of different messages. The optical telescope was destroyed during the war of 1808-9, but replaced immediately after the resumption of Swedish-Russian relations.

It was from the coast of Eckerö that the route between Åland and the west was consolidated when the province became a part of the Russian Grand Duchy. The first substantial building constructed in Åland in the Russian period was the neo-classical customs house, designed by C. F. Engel, principal architect of early Helsinki, and dated 1826. It remains one of the two most impressive buildings in Eckerö parish. In it were advertised the varying ferry charges: winter rates from Martinmass in November until Easter, spring rates from Easter until the break-up of ice, summer rates until Michaelmas. Here, too, were listed the licensed innkeepers and posthouses. Eckerö was to remain a principal route of entry into Åland until Mariehamn was founded in the 1860s.

THE FLEET AND THE FERRY BOATS

Meanwhile, from the late 1830s, the first steamboats entered Ålandic waters for the summer season. *Prince Menschikoff*, its paddles turning in leisurely fashion, its stove-pipe chimney dispensing wood smoke, its passage interrupted when twilight fell, plied between Stockholm and St Petersburg by way of Åland. *Storfursten* operated from Stockholm by way of Degerby to Åbo. Once Mariehamn was established as a port, the links to Åbo were strengthened. In 1866, *Admiral von Platen* called on its maiden voyage from Stockholm to Åbo. Fifty-two Ålanders, mostly of the local quality, took their first trip on this 'floating hotel' at 10 knots an hour. The captains on these early steamships maintained a pleasantly informal relationship with life ashore. It was their business, for example, to order horse transport for passengers at their points of disembarkation.

The fleet of local steamships that came into service to form the principal links between the main islands after 1890 operated widely until after World War II. Vessels such as *Åland* and *Viola* were attractive, all-purpose ships, of several hundred tons burden, transporting cargo of every kind as well as passengers and animals. Save in winter, they performed the role of local carrier, bus service, milk lorry and post van combined. They formed a part of the two dozen archipelago steamships that had their terminus under the black sails of Åbo's windmills on the Aura river. Changes in population distribution, the development of the large ferry, of bridges, buses and private motor boats, have either driven them out of service or called for state subsidies to keep them in operation to meet social needs.

Page 143 (*above*) Midsummer Eve: in most villages a maypole decorated with leaves is raised, around which people dance to the tunes of traditional songs;
(*right*) the celebration of the fiftieth anniversary of the autonomy of Åland at the statue of Julius Sundblom

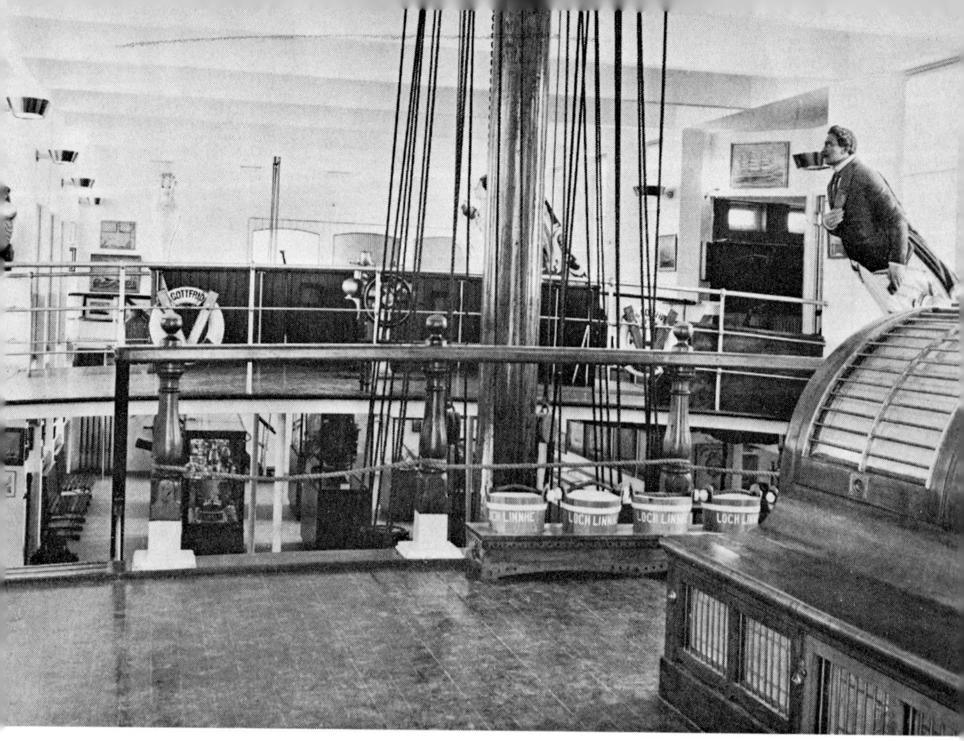

Page 144 (*above*) The Maritime Museum at Mariehamn. Complete sections of windjammers make the museum of outstanding interest for visitors; (*below*) pike fishing is a favourite pastime for Ålanders and visitors alike

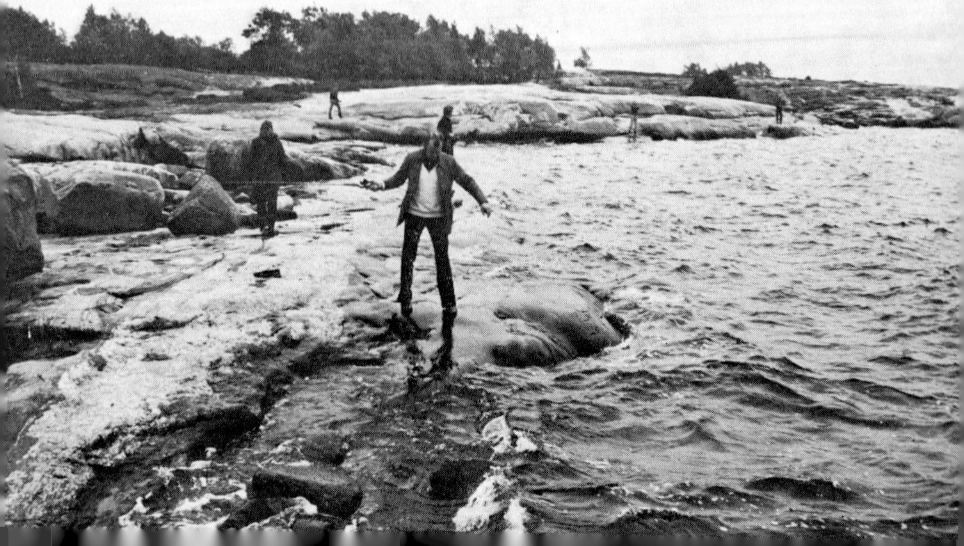

It is less than a century since experiments with continuous winter steamer services between Finland and Sweden were first made. There are Ålanders still living who could have taken the ice boat over the historic Signildskär route or the 75km horse-and-sleigh ride to Stockholm. In the later 1870s, experiments in winter shipping between Sweden, south-west Finland and Estonia were made, but direct winter links between Sweden and Åland were not attempted until 1887. The Åland Steamship Company, which came into being in that year, tried to maintain a winter service with its steamship *Åland* between the Swedish coast and the main island, but the vessel stuck in the ice during the first January of its operation. Even *Sofia*, a ship which A. E. Nordenskiöld had used on expeditions to both Spitsbergen and Greenland, and Finland's first real winter vessel, suffered the ignominy of being laid up during the first year that it took to the Stockholm-Mariehamn–Åbo route in 1894. By the late 1890s, the first ice-breaker became available to aid vessels in the Åland Sea and, within a decade, the ice-breaker *Skiftet* had been recruited for Ålandic service. After World War II, Åland acquired a special ice-strengthened ship to guarantee connections in winter. *Aranda* operates as a research vessel in summer time. Yet, for all its difficulties with ice, Åland has to be seen in its Finnish perspectives as one of the most climatically favoured parts of the country. As a result, the potentialities of Mariehamn as a winter outport for Finland were discussed on a number of occasions in former times. Among schemes was one for an Åland railway to be tied by rail ferry to Nystad (F. Uusikaupunki) on the south-western Finnish mainland.

The modern ferries that tie Åland to east and west are of about 5–6,000 gross registered tons, and have cabin or deck accommodation for 1,000–2,000 passengers. They are ice-strengthened and capable of functioning throughout the year, though the entire fleet only operates during the summer. Mariehamn receives the staggering total of 170 tourist ferries a

I   145 week in the summer and over seventy of these belong to one Ålandic line. In the far west, with the restoration of the historic post route to Grisslehamn, Eckerö has taken on a new lease of life as a ferry port.

The ferries are only one component of the modern fleet. In 1973, Åland's shipowners' association listed sixty-nine ships with a gross registered tonnage of 428,317 tons. Most vessels were either regular line cargo vessels or moderately sized cargo ships engaged in charter trade. There was one tanker exceeding 100,000 tons. Control of the fleet was vested in fourteen principal companies, though some of these only operated one ship. Åland companies have been accustomed to buying up shipping in the world market, and a recent purchase of two cruise ships of 10,000 tons each illustrates a new line of development. On the other hand, the purchase of new vessels directly from the ship-yard is increasingly the practice. It is reflected in the steadily falling age of the Ålandic mercantile marine. The crews that man the fleet are no longer predominantly Ålanders.

THE FISHERIES

The character of the Ålandic fishing industry has changed fundamentally in recent years. There are still hundreds of wooden boats, mostly undecked, based on rock-rimmed harbours beside which crouch red-painted boathouses as big as barns. But fishing operations have been given a new flexibility by two contrasting developments. The first has been the replacement of large, expensive and collectively owned nets (locally known as *notar*) by smaller, cheaper and individually owned drift nets (called *krokskötar*). The second has been the rise of the trawler fleet. Åland's fifty-five trawlers represent about a third of Finland's total. They are usually steel-hulled and are generally operated by two or three men. They account for the greater part of the fish landed. In contrast to the smaller boats, they operate throughout the year, largely outside territorial

146

waters. A trawler can return from a six-hour operation with an average catch of several tons of herrings; a good catch may be as large as 7–8 tons.

As the changes have taken place, many of the old-established rhythms of the fishing activity have been relinquished. For example, seasonal migrations to the fishing camps in the skerries are disappearing and the collections of cabins are being steadily deserted. Ören in Kökar, used since the Middle Ages, had some 300 people employing its assemblage of forty buildings fifty years ago; it is now rarely occupied. Picturesque harbours, such as Käringsund (in Eckerö) and Bovik (in Hammarland), which were living expressions of fishing and boatbuilding forty years ago, have become museum areas. But although techniques and practices have changed, fishing remains a strongly seasonal pursuit. This characteristic is imparted by the herring fisheries which reach a climax in late summer and early autumn. The *strömming* or Baltic herring, which accounts for 90 per cent of the catch, lies behind some of the oldest exporting activities of the Ålanders. Historic practices, such as the movement of herring men (and their wives) to Helsinki and Stockholm, continue, though they are accompanied by new ones consequent upon the extension of the season and the larger scale of operations.

An immediate problem of the larger catch is that Åland has insufficient processing plants to handle it. Its total cold storage capacity is 300 tons, while its refrigerating equipment can only handle 30 tons a day. In addition to the sales of fresh fish and smoked herring to mainland Sweden and Finland, the canneries produce a range of familiar pickled and spiced fillets which are essential to any Scandinavian cold table. But the principal consumers of herring are not now human, they are farm-bred mink. Today, the price of Åland's harvest of the sea is a response to the needs of the mink and changes in the world price of ranch-mink furs. The old-established but more expensive winter operation of trawling (with the aid of a tractor) through ice holes is still practised locally.

There are other fish beside herring in the seas that surround Åland. Principal among them is the salmon, the annual catch of which is 3–400 tons. It is sold fresh or salted; *gravlax*, as it is called when salted, is a speciality of the inner Baltic. A limited amount is smoked, an eighteen-hour process. The salmon is highly sensitive to sea temperatures and its presence or absence is conditioned by the whole range of seasonal circumstances. Lavaret (a white fish of the salmon family known in Swedish as *sik*), perch and pike are next in importance, while salmon trout, cod, flat fish and eel are more restricted in their occurrence. The largest fish caught annually are recorded in the island's newspaper—salmon exceeding 20kg, salmon trout of 10kg, pike of 12kg and lavaret of 5kg are not unusual. Because of their sensitivity, the threat of over-fishing and the depredations of the seal, salmon are now cultivated on a fish farm at Guttorp in Sund. Over 100,000 salmon fry are released from it each year. There is also cultivation of pike, rainbow trout and sea trout.

The degree of dependence on fishing differs considerably from place to place and is changing in its incidence. There are 794 names on the fishermen's list and 331 part-time operators. The outer islands—Brändö, Föglö, Kökar and Kumlinge—contribute 45 per cent of the fishermen. One problem is that, with the growth in size of trawlers, many smaller harbours are inadequate. Only six harbours can satisfactorily accommodate the trawlers and they are all on the main island. Full-time fishermen work on an average 177 days a year, 56 of which are in winter months; part-time fishermen, 61 days, 33 of which are in winter.

Åland has another fish harvest—partly fresh-water—the crayfish. In recent years, crayfish in Sweden and on the Finnish mainland have been subject to disease and substantial diminution in numbers. Åland's crayfish stocks, although healthy, are vulnerable to over-fishing. The crayfish harvest begins in Åland before that in Sweden and the tourist invasion increases the pressure on a limited resource. It is difficult to estimate the catch, but it is between 36,000–49,000 a year. What was once the peasant's perquisite has become a gastronomic luxury.

SAGA OF THE SQUARE RIGGERS

From 1880 until the eve of World War I, Åland had a fleet of more than 200 sailing vessels. As the period of locally owned and operated vessels declined, that of the sailing ship had its final flowering. The very facts that spelt the demise of the small sailing cargo vessel gave momentary respite to Åland's ship owners. With the rise of the steamship, they capitalised on the falling price of sailing ships, bought a fleet and continued to run it with apparent profit.

In the twenty years preceding World War I, they purchased no fewer than thirty-seven windjammers. Most of them had been constructed in Scottish or English wharves and had sailed in the company of tea clippers and wool clippers that had brought fame to their owners. The Ålandic fleet suffered cruelly during World War I, when such impressive sailing vessels as *Borrowdale* and *Frieda* were torpedoed. Immediately afterwards, however, Åland ship owners re-entered the market and were buying up superannuated fully-rigged vessels which might otherwise have gone to the scrap-yard. Gustav Erikson led the purchasers; in 1921, for example, this latter-day sea king became the owner of two vessels which were both to claim world attention. *Herzogin Cecilia* was bought for £4,250; *Passat*, for £4,000— 'rag and bone prices', in the words of Pamela Eriksson. By the late 1920s, the name of Mariehamn was being carried round the world as the port of registration of the world's last sailing fleet. In 1928, the fleet included 21 iron- and steel-plated sailing ships, 4 wooden barques, 33 schooners and 11 motor sailing ships. They amounted to less than 50,000 tons altogether, but they were a unique collection. The ships were divided into a Baltic fleet and a high seas fleet. Vessels of the high seas fleet

149

bore names that were to rival in international renown those of popular liners and warships. To sound the fanfare of their names —as Sally Salminen put it in her memoirs—is to conjure up adventure; best known were *Pamir, L'Avenir, Moshulu, Viking, Penang, Pommern, Hougomont, Olivebank, Lawhill* and *Archibald Russell*. All of these ships were about 2,500 net registered tons, about 90m long, 13·5m wide, and with masts which towered 30m above their decks.

Some indication of the routes followed and cargoes carried is provided by listing a decade of major runs from the log book of *Pommern*. In 1923, the vessel sailed from Iquiqui to Bruges with a cargo of saltpetre; in 1924, from Iquiqui to Antwerp, with saltpetre; in 1925, from Larvik to Melbourne, with timber; in 1926, from Newcastle, NSW, to Callao, with coal; in 1927, from Tacoma to Natal, with timber; in 1928, from Liverpool to Sydney, with rock salt, and then from Sydney to Birkenhead, with wheat; in 1929, from Larvik to Melbourne, with timber; in 1931, from South Australia to Cork, with wheat; and in 1932, from South Australia to Glasgow, with wheat.

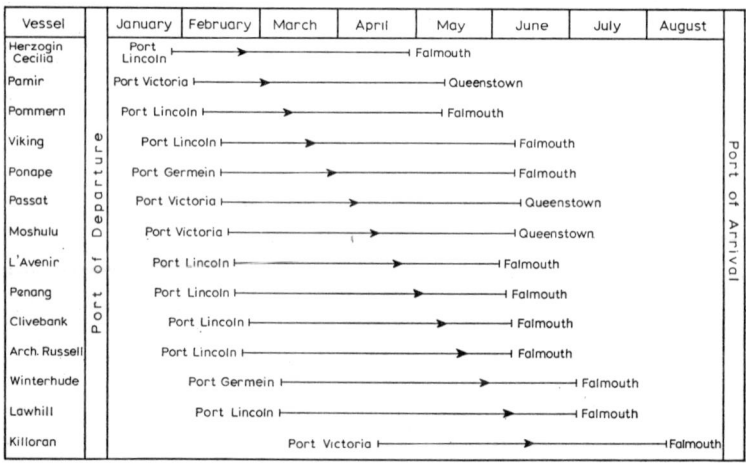

The 'Great Grain Race', 1935

The climax of the Erikson experience came in the 1930s when the grain race from Spencer Gulf to British landfalls made annual newspaper headlines. The diagram opposite provides the timetable for 1935. Anything less than 100 days was regarded as a fast trip, though no Erikson ships approached the speed of *Lightning* which ran from Melbourne to Liverpool in sixty-four days. On the Australian run, the average amount of grain carried was 4,000 tons and, having delivered their cargoes to British or Irish terminals, a fair number of vessels put into Mariehamn's west harbour for summer leave.

Ålanders who sailed before the mast are still to be found, surrounded by the souvenirs and trophies of half a century of sea-going. On their seamen's chests sit models of the ships in which they sailed. Around them are ostrich eggs and sea porcupines, coral fans and conch shells (lichened conch shells also lie upon seamen's headstones in the churchyards). Above them hang portraits of idle ships upon painted oceans (ship portraiture was almost an industry for such London artists as T. G. Purvis and A. V. Gregory). Sepia photographs in seashell frames commemorate ancestors who had exchanged their boots and sou'westers for stove-pipe hats and frock coats while cargoes were unloaded in Hull or Hamburg, Antwerp or Nantes. Ålanders are able to reminisce in languages other than their mother tongue. *Mother Sea* and its sequel *Pulley-Haul* by Elis Karlsson are among the most remarkable records to come out of Åland and they were written in English. Their author, a latter-day Henry Dana, was not only able to capture all the moods of the ocean but was also equipped to pronounce on every detail of the furnishing and behaviour of a ship at sea. Karlsson was no adventurer participating for the sake of the experience in the grain races, but a sober mariner whose life and livelihood were written in salt water. His experiences complement those of Eric Newby's *Last Grain Race*. Nor are the records of the considerable number of passengers who joined the fleet (and qualified for the Cape Horner's Club) able to express the responses of the regular sailors. For all its choruses of sea shanties and flights of albatrosses, life on a windjammer was exhaustingly arduous and infinitely monotonous—'like the second day of creation for weeks on end', commented one mariner. Another concluded that there were only two happy moments on a trip—'sailing into harbour and sailing out of it'.

Fate overtook the Erikson sailing fleet in a variety of ways. *Penang* disappeared completely on her way from Port Lincoln to Cork. *Olivebank* hit a mine and sank in the North Sea. *Passat* and *Pamir* were sold to a Belgian collector. *Herzogin Cecilia*, the flagship and pride of the family, was wrecked in 1936 with a broken keel near Bolt Head in Devon. *Viking* became a museum ship in Göteborg. *Archibald Russell* went to the breaker's yard in 1948. *Moshulu* was converted into a luxury inn off Los Angeles. *Pommern*, a four-mast barque built in Glasgow in 1903 and carefully restored in the shipyards of Åbo, has become the distinguishing tourist feature of Mariehamn. It is a ghost ship, with its twenty-eight sails permanently furled and its great echoing hold void of the mountains of grain that were its historic cargo. The blueprints for its construction, down to the detail of its standing and running rigging, are in the adjacent nautical museum. They are watched over by the golden-haired, blue-draped lady who was the figurehead of the barque *Amanda*, the white-draped lady from *Loch Linne* and the choker-collared Walter Wilson from *California*. The museum is an apotheosis of all that has gone into Ålandic shipping, with the treasures of several generations of seamen—sextants, chronometers and star globes—and the ponderous reminders of their hard labours, from *Hougomont*'s smithy to *Viking*'s sail-sewing machine.

The sailing fleet has been dispersed, but contemporary Åland has a larger fleet than at any time in its history, and it is mostly in the hands of the families that owned the square-rig vessels. Mariehamn is the principal beneficiary of this enterprise and it is estimated that more than 40 per cent of its income derives from its shipping interests. In 1972, it received 6,254 vessels (4,444 in 1971), with a gross registered tonnage of 8,570,000. The growth in the volume of shipping using Mariehamn has called for major changes in the handling facilities of its quays. The waterfront of its western harbour has been fundamentally changed to meet the needs of its passenger traffic. In the process problems of discrimination have emerged between the Åland ferry fleet and ferries belonging to mainland companies.

SHIPWRECKS AND SMUGGLING

For many, life afloat has been the prelude to death at sea. As the framed paintings of one proud vessel after another sail round living-room walls on summer seas, it is necessary to reflect upon the roll call of shipwrecks that is the reverse side of the coin. The number of ships lost in storms or sunk in war is long and depressing. They are vessels with brave names—*Angela* and *Alexander*, *Libanon* and *Cedna*, *North Star* and *Virgo*. Many have unknown graves. Those cast upon Ålandic shores are usually commemorated with memorials, such as that to the barque *Plus* on Hertron kobb. The windy churchyard of Kökar bears the headstones of men from many nations whose ships have foundered in its treacherous skerries. Other stones have been erected to those swept overboard or those who have fallen from giddy rigging on the high seas. Each year takes its toll of fishermen in home waters. Dödmansskär—dead man's skerry—is a place name which occurs more than once in the islands. The skerries are scattered with memorial cairns and sometimes, as on Rannö, with more formal monuments. In the quiet of a summer day, a little armada of mourning fishing boats, motor boats and yachts may push out to the presumed site where a winter storm overwhelmed a vessel. A memorial service will be held, ribboned wreaths cast upon the waters and a stone erected on the nearest rocky outcrop by the fishermen's cooperative society. Out of such experiences are created the semi-autobiographical novels of Anni Blomqvist, whose home background is the island of Simskäla in north Vårdö.

The reverse of losses at sea have been the finds of the beachcombers. In earlier times, strandings and wrecks were prized for the contributions they made to local coffers. The Ålandic aphorism, 'The Lord blesses the coast', has an ironic ring today. Never was more flotsam cast upon the coasts of Åland; never was so much of it of so little value, never was it so resistant to the cleansing action of the waves.

Nor is it surprising that the maritime acumen of the Ålanders should here and there, from time to time, be turned to less virtuous activities. In early days, Åland had its sea robbers—Stigmanhamn in Föglö is a place name reminiscent of them. More regularly it has fostered smugglers, the particular items of whose trade have been responsive to customs regulations. The archipelago is well-nigh incapable of surveillance by customs authorities. Brandy, coffee, syrup and wool yarn seem relatively harmless commodities by comparison with products moved during the years of Russian oppression, when Åland doubtless had its gun runners. Certainly, gun running occurred elsewhere around the Finnish archipelagos and the Russian navy sought to restrict it in Åland by sending survey units to work there. Against the background of liquor licensing introduced by Sweden in 1917, and Finland's prohibition experiment between 1919 and 1932, the islands found themselves central to the trading in illicit spirits that was conducted with foreign vessels outside territorial waters. The *Sprittider* is still recalled in Åland, and relics of it, such as the special containers for smuggling spirits, have become museum specimens. But, as ever, it was the Ålanders who took the risks and the black marketeers of the cities who made the profit. The sale of alcoholic beverages, is still restricted to Mariehamn. Åland, as part of Finland, shares the state alcohol monopoly. Distribution is from a single, central store, though beer may now be purchased from the village shop.

A second climax of smuggling occurred during World War II and in the lean days that followed, when the islanders contrived to obtain an immense range of goods for transmission to rationed Finland. In the process, strange double standards of morality were erected, and ready cash in hard currency gathered under the most unlikely roofs. Åland has rarely been without an element of the picaresque somewhere in its make-up.

THE SHIP AS SYMBOL

The ship is symbolic of Åland—from boat-shaped burial sites, through the votive vessels that hang in its churches (the oldest from the 1680s), the 4,000 taxed pleasure boats, the fleet of rainbow-coloured ferries to the ocean-going carriers. Like the Faroese, the Ålanders have made a maritime impact out of all proportion to their numbers. The web of its maritime connections never meant more to them than today. It has been through shipping and maritime circumstance that Europe has been made aware of Åland. For these reasons, there are more references to it in international literature than to any of Finland's other provinces. Yachtsmen have visited Ålandic waters for over a century. They probably made their debut in 1854 to witness the attack on Bomarsund. During the inter-war years, K. Adlard Cole's *Mary Anne* logged a cruise among the 'thousand' islands which was complemented by Peter Pye's appropriately named yachting experience, *A Sail in the Forest*. The islands have become a summer playground for a multitude of yachtsmen from Sweden and Finland, as well as farther afield. But it was the obsequies that accompanied the last days of the sailing fleet that placed Åland and the Ålanders most firmly on the mental map of the world. There is an air of finality about the literature that it called forth: *The Last of the Square-rigged Ships* (F. Ferrell Cotton), *Square Riggers, The Final Epoch 1921–58* (A. A. Hurst), *The Last of the Windjammers* (Basil Lubbock), *The Tall Ships Pass* (W. L. A. Derby), *Falmouth for Orders* (the story of the last clipper ship race around Cape Horn by the most prolific contributor on the age of sail, A. J. Villiers).

Such a fleet had need of agents, especially in London, which was then the world's centre of maritime chartering. It was through H. Clarkson and Co that many younger enthusiasts made their acquaintance with the square riggers; in the 1930s, they advertised 'long voyages to Australia at ten shillings a day' on them. It was also possible to join the vessels as they returned from British ports to Mariehamn, provided passengers were prepared to do without the services of stewards and stewardesses, and brought their own supplies of wine and spirits. To Clarkson's city office also came the Ålander, Matti Ingman, who became a legendary figure in his own right. A bookish shipper, he haunted auction sales and bought volumes by the thousand to send to Finnish libraries. He also succeeded in negotiating the return to Åland of the big bell of Skarpans which had sat silent in the Tower of London since it had been brought there as a trophy following the British naval assault in 1854.

Other elegies might be written on Åland's shipping. Two generations ago, wooden three-masted barques were still leaving the stocks in the wharves of Lemland, Saltvik and Jomala. Today, orders for ships are placed by Ålanders in the yards of many nations and are a not unimportant element in domestic politics. The same applies to the maintenance of Ålandic shipping. Because of the shortage of skilled labour in Åland, there has been Ålandic investment in the repair yards of Nystad. Even Åland's 5,000 ton floating dock generates its own particular stresses. For, in the world of shipping, economy and society also conflict. To lift a 10,000 ton vessel above the horizon of Mariehamn's waterfront is to destroy a tourist amenity and reduce its aesthetic appeal. At the same time, the dock diversifies Åland's employment structure in a town which tourism is destroying as fast as it creates anew. Argument and counter-argument—all eventually return to the sea and its ships.

Navigare necesse est is inscribed upon the memorial to the

Erikson family in Mariehamn cemetery. A steersman at the wheel is its emblem. Flanking headstones have been raised to ship's captains, customs officers, pilots and lighthouse keepers—all proudly identified according to their calling. The polished marble bears the motifs of their daily lives—lighthouses, anchors, pole-stars, seagulls and the square rigger in full sail. In all, there is an echo of the epitaph for *Brother Killian*, hero of Valdemar Nyman's medieval Ålandic romance:

In the sea is salvation; in the sea is fulfilment.

9 THE FORTUNATE ISLES

ÅLANDERS have inherited a world of islands, an archipelago of archipelagos. In European terms, the inheritance may be modest, for its landscapes lack drama and its resources are limited. But, if it is *nuances* which count in the appreciation of the Fennoscandian scene, it is the extended range of these *nuances* that distinguishes Åland. And the people have explored and employed to the full the possibilities that they represent. At the same time, despite an apparent sturdiness and robustness, Åland and its people are inherently sensitive. The inheritance of Åland is precariously maintained. Its flora and fauna, for all their spring and summer exuberance, are held in an extremely critical balance. Economy and society increasingly resemble them in the delicacy of their adjustment. Åland needs protection from too much intrusion if the characteristics of its natural and human landscapes are to be maintained. Plant and bird communities require a measure of defence against mounting pressures. So, too, do the customs and traditions that Ålanders have inherited and which add piquancies to their daily life.

It is ironical that Åland, having rejected both east and west politically (and having acquired the respect of east and west as a result) should find itself confronted with a new system of pressures which threaten its identity. Principal among them is the tourist invasion, an experience which has brought Åland under the sway of its neighbours as never before. It poses a dilemma because its consequences are not immediately observable and because it yields handsome financial returns. Through tourism, it would be all too easy for the islands to gain the benefits of the whole material world and in the process to lose their soul.

External pressures have also made Ålanders increasingly conscious of their provincial identity and of the differences within their island home. Its unitary character, suggested by the map or by the aerial photograph, dissolves on the ground. The characteristics and qualities that distinguish the whole are shared by all the component parts of Åland, but the combinations of the characteristics shift and change. Although Åland has always been an assemblage of little Ålands, the need to recognise this fact and to respond to its consequences has only become manifest in recent years. The fact that Åland consists of a mainland group of parishes (the *Innandels*) and an island group (the *Utandels*) has new overtones as well as old undertones. The western 'mainlanders' react differently from the eastern 'islanders' (the inhabitants of Brändö, Föglö, Kumlinge, Kökar, Sottunga and Vårdö). Föglö, Sottunga and Vårdö have had sufficient coherence to acquire the epithet *Sunnandels*, the southern parishes. These distinctions are important because they have bred and continue to breed different attitudes to life. Modern economists talk of the leading and the lagging areas in the archipelago. For the naturalists, the lagging areas are not infrequently the areas of refuge. Accordingly, different parts of Åland need different kinds of treatment.

The characteristics of the different parts have been exaggerated by three processes which have affected and continue to affect Åland powerfully—migration, emigration and the seasonal invasion of tourists. All three processes make for instability—exaggerating the contrast between the rural and the urban (as expressed by Mariehamn) and between the deserted winter countryside and its locally crowded summer occupation. In turn, urbanisation and tourism make manifest the deficiencies of the home province and the superfluities that appear to characterise the adjacent metropolitan areas of Sweden and Finland. It is ironical that while many Ålandic realists migrate to the mainland to escape the apparent restraints of their home islands, a steady stream of mainland romanticists moves in to escape from metropolitan pressures.

Skärgårdsland—schlaraffenland (island world—dreamland): in such terms, literary romanticists have been extolling the appeal of the islands for over a century. Zachris Topelius sought summer inspiration among islands which to him were 'nature's green thoughts in a haven of blue waves'. August Strindberg found mental harmony in what he called the *intermezzo scherzando* of the neighbouring Stockholm archipelago. In his lighter moments, Valdemar Nyman sees Åland as 'L'île féerique'; in his more serious moods, he regards its islands as a refuge: '*Ö i havet för en Robinson, alltid rädda sig Gud upp på en ö i havet*' (an island in the sea for a Robinson, God always saves by throwing up an island in the sea). But escapists who once found their

. . . island rare,
Far from mankind, and seeming far from care

on the doorsteps of their town or city homes, must now push farther afield. As a result the Åland archipelago has been caught in the net of those who are casting for the solitudes and simplicities of a deserted island. At the same time, those who are not fortunate enough to acquire their own plots and their own increasingly swift means of transport to them, are propelled by a sense of curiosity to see what they are missing. So, too, are those lured by such works of art as Roland Klang's sculptural fantasy of the archipelago, commissioned by Ålands Bank, and converted into one of Scandinavia's most beguiling posters.

CUSTOM AND TRADITION

Custom and tradition invest any area with a measure of romance, and by their very nature, isolated islands tend to protect past practices and ideas. Åland's social practices, as with its social institutions, tend to be rooted in Sweden in general and in the province of Uppland in particular.

Christmas day (*Jul dag*), with its spruce trees, candles, Father Christmas, pike-ham-and-rice-porridge dinner, is anticipated by the Little Christmas celebration on the first Sunday in Advent. On 13 December, Lucia—*die beata Lucia virginis*—makes her appearance, wearing a crown of lighted candles, surrounded by her white-robed attendants. She rivals Father Christmas in the impact she makes on Mariehamn, where she becomes the subject of a procession through the streets. St Stephen (Staffan, to Ålanders) is increasingly recalled, with his star boys and his mummer's play. Twelfth Night is also an occasion for parties. The Feast of the Annunciation (*Maria bebådelsedag*) brings a public holiday. By Good Friday (*Lång-fredag*) birch branches have been pampered into mouse-ear leaf and, decorated with brightly dyed feathers, announce the season of Easter eggs. The next public holiday falls soon after. It is May Day, preceded by Valborgsmäss, a traditional evening for students throughout Scandinavia and an evening when bonfires used to be lit in Åland. All Saints' Day (*Alla helgons dag*) is also a public holiday.

The most distinctive traditional feature of Åland is the midsummer pole—*Majstången*. Although midsummer poles appear to be an old-established feature of the Åland scene, little attention was paid to them by earlier travellers. The Finnish Archaeological Society, on its first formal visit to Åland in 1871, immediately called attention to the poles, recording several in every hamlet, each more elaborate than the last. Today, more than fifty are erected in the summer; they may be 10m high, with as many as six transverse arms. Spiders' webs of threads, on which aspen leaves have been knotted, are strung between them. Their garlanded, wreathed and flagged frames are crowned with wooden figures in folk costumes, ships, cocks, suns or pennants. To lift and secure them in a vertical position

K   161 is a craft in itself—and an important one, because the poles, as they wither and decay in the autumn and winter gales, constitute a local hazard for which the community bears responsibility.

The resuscitation of the midsummer pole is part and parcel of the romantic interest in folk culture that reached Åland from mainland Scandinavia in the late nineteenth century. It goes with the revival of folk dancing—from the ring dances with their sung accompaniments, through the set dances for which the fiddler provides the tune, to the popular dances for which the concertina comes into its own. A fiddlers' guild, which has held competitions since 1907, has published six volumes of traditional bridal marches, waltzes and polkas. As in the rest of Scandinavia, folk costumes have been revived—early nineteenth-century conceits which are worn willingly by most women and reluctantly by most men. Åland offers at least one seamen's song—*Båklandets Vackra Maja*, with words by Arvid Mörne—which has made an international mark.

But Ålandic folk culture is of more than popular status. It is the object of academic inquiry and, since it contributes to the individuality of Åland, it acquires a politico-social significance. *Svensk Literatursällskapet*, the literary society of the Swedish-speaking minority in Finland, includes Åland as part of its domain. Accordingly, Åland figures in the studies of folk life—customs, songs, tales, poems and dialect variations—which the society initiates. Even children's games are included in their collections. Counting games such as the untranslatable jingle recorded in Lappo on the island of Brändö have their origins in the Dark Ages.

> Anntän, dänntänn
> Meetika männtänn
> Liischa Laascha loo
> Ooken pooken
> Töjmista kooken
> Piff, paff, uut

At an academic level, Ålanders have established their own research series—*Ålands Kulturstiftelse* and *Åländska Handlingar*. For two generations they have supported *Åland*, an annual publication devoted to the spread of knowledge about the province. *St Olof*, sponsored by the church, has a similar purpose. While it is the function of the state to maintain the fabric of Finland's churches, and while the national museum's authority administers a grant to historical monuments, such as Kastelholm, local organisations have found plenty of scope for their surplus energies in collecting material for the folk museums of Jan Karls gården, an eighteenth-century farmhouse reassembled in the castle grounds. Åland museum complements the enterprise of the shipping fraternity with its maritime museum, while the private collection of bygones has given rise to local museums at Äppelö in north Hammarland, Norrgårds in Saltvik's Syllöda and Labbas in Eckerö. Encouragement of concern for vernacular architecture has been another aim of the local societies. They have been conspicuously successful in arousing interest in the islands' windmills, of which more than 1,000 were listed at the turn of the century. Among examples of excellent restoration are those at Frebbenby in Saltvik, Seffers in Gottby and Andersböle in Jomala. The Åland branch of the Martha Society, founded before World War I, encourages traditional arts and crafts and the practice of old customs. Wedding poles are still erected at the homes of bridal pairs in country districts, though less than formerly do they remain until the birth of the first child. Small spruce trees traditionally occupy the four corners of a hearse as it journeys to the immaculately kept churchyard, where headstones still announce the professions of the departed—*Fiskaren, Skepparen, Bonden*.

But it is matters of life rather than death which are the concern of the Martha societies. They propagate the virtues of traditional foods, such as black bread, pancakes, salted fish, rose-hip soup, bath house-smoked ham (now an industry in its own right) and the sweet cheese prepared from the first milk taken from the cow after calving. It is their disciples who follow in the culinary wake of the hunters and shooters, for the 3,000 sportsmen who participate in the springtime bird shoot, and especially the duck shoot, require the services of dressers and cooks (not least to prepare the duck soup). The autumn elk shoot, recalling the royal hunts that characterised Åland in Swedish times, takes place in October and November. Hare hunting still excites some countryfolk in February and March. Crayfish netting begins in late July, when there is enough darkness to enable candles and coloured lanterns to create a festive atmosphere. Not surprisingly, all this activity provides trophies throughout the year sufficient to keep a thriving taxidermist industry alive in the islands.

On all social occasions, as is the practice throughout Scandinavia, flags flutter freely. In Åland, it is the blue, yellow and red Ålandic flag—even on 6 December, which is Finland's independence day and a public holiday. Åland has initiated its own flag day—the last Sunday in April—which provides the formal opportunity for a display of provincial patriotism.

THE TOURIST EXPLOSION

Holidaymakers have been coming to Åland for nearly a century, though it was not until 1889 that the first bathers came for their cures. The earliest holidaymakers included tourists from Imperial Russia as well as from Finland, for Åland was the farthest point west that they could travel without special permission. In a minor way, Åland became a summer haunt of merchants, senior army officers, even princes. The visits of the Emperor Alexander III and his Empress Maria in 1893 and 1894 in the royal yacht *Zarevna* lent a cachet to the islands which lingered for a long time. Kejsarhamnen—the emperor's harbour—was the epithet used for Bomarsund's harbour among the older generation. Largely in response to the summer demand a forty-room hotel, complete with an 'inhalatorium', was opened in Mariehamn in 1900; it was accidentally burned by Russian soldiers in 1916. The spacious wooden *Societetshuset* was its successor. In country districts, unpretentious *pensionats* were established. Most of these old clapboard buildings with their fretwork ornamentation remain, some still retaining in their lounges the pleasing bric-à-brac and uncomfortably solid furniture that characterised the St Petersburg as well as the Stockholm of their day.

But if tourism is nothing new for Åland, the scale of its recent development is staggering. Within the space of a generation, the number of visitors has leapt from a few thousands to a million. More than three-quarters of the summer visitors are Swedish, though the number of other nationals increases rapidly. The summer invasion consists of three different types of visitor. First, there are the birds of passage who come for the day to shop in Mariehamn; they total about 800,000. Secondly, there are those who stay at hotels or come with cars and tents to occupy the camping sites; they account for about 200,000 of the total. Thirdly, there are the longer-term residents, who either own or lease summer cabins. They also purchase or rent abandoned farmhouses—and rescue them from their picturesque slumdom.

The invasion is inseparable from the fact that during the last generation, metropolitan Finland and the Stockholm area have become two of Scandinavia's most intensive areas of growth, affluence and consumption. They are only a few hours' distant and Åland falls in the orbit of their influence. While they have drawn Ålanders away from their less developed homeland, the very land that they desert opens up new opportunities for Finns and Swedes who have begun to exhaust the recreational opportunities of their own archipelagos.

Many Scandinavian visitors accept Åland for what it is— unsophisticated recreation land. They do not want bright lights; the light nights have appeal enough. They choose to become children of nature for a few brief weeks and seek the summer

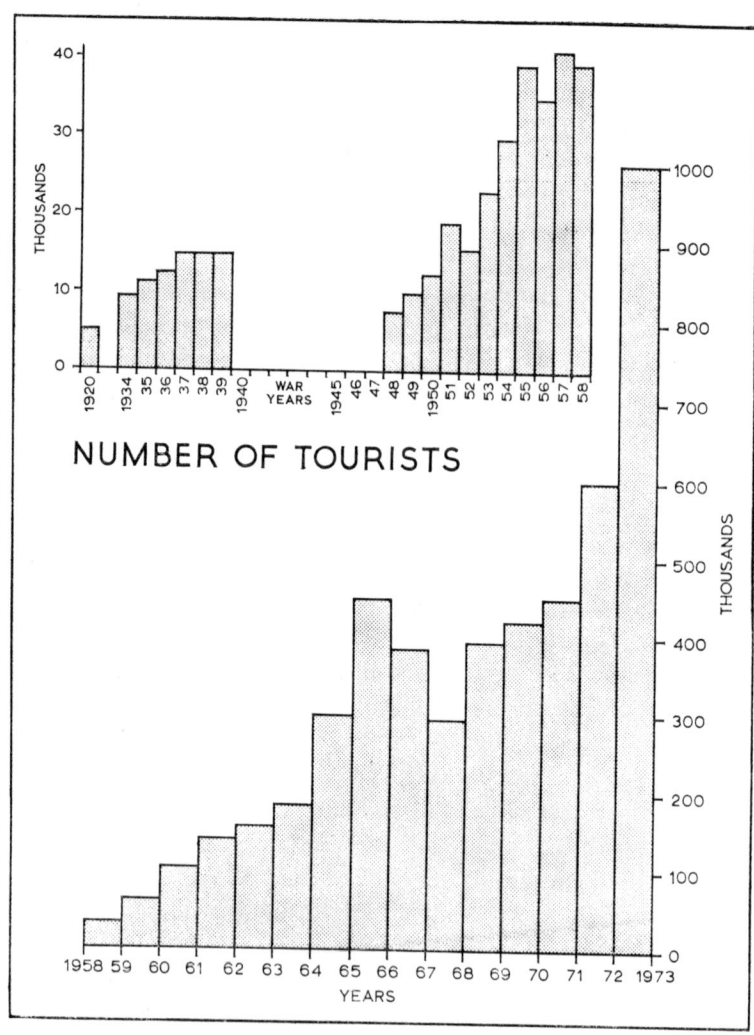

The growth of the tourist trade

solitudes across the narrows of the Åland Sea or Skiftet. But the growth in their numbers, the changing nature of many of their demands—not to speak of the induced demands—give rise to increasing apprehension.

The tourist explosion, which can bring both fortune and misfortune, raises a number of questions. First, it is not of Mediterranean magnitude, simply because the season is limited. Hotel construction, even with an eye to conferences, is relatively risky. Of considerable prospective importance—especially in view of population forecasts of 2 million for the Stockholm area by the year 2000—is the provision of summer cabins and camping sites. It is principally coastal sites which visitors are seeking and Åland has extensive coasts. But, by the time that water supply (deficiency of which is a regular occurrence), sanitation, existing occupation, conservation, fire risks (forest fires appear to multiply with tourist numbers) and physical undesirability have been considered, suitable areas are relatively limited. For rented cabins and camping sites, concentration favours the provision of services; this is encouraged by the provincial government with financial incentives.

Argument continues as to whether cabins should be sold or rented. Many farmers and fisherfolk see in summer visitors a profitable means of disposing of profitless property. Uncontrolled development can make for social difficulties as occupation is intensified. At present, for example, Lemland parish has no major difficulties, but the nature of its development illustrates a potential problem. In 1972 permanent residents totalled 700; resident summer immigrants, 850. The situation is partly held in check by Ålandic property laws. Since 1951, formal public advertisement has been required of all applications by non-residents to purchase land or buildings in Åland. Any Ålander wishing to take advantage of his right of pre-emption is given thirty days in which to lodge a claim. If he is then prepared to pay a sum equal to that offered by the purchaser, an agreed time is allotted in which he can arrange a purchase. After the expiry of this time, the sale becomes valid. The five-year residence for provincial qualification as an Ålander also exerts a restraining influence on purchases by outsiders.

Developers are confronted with an increasingly powerful conservation lobby. Two generations ago, Ålanders began to concern themselves with the preservation of flora and fauna. Today, thanks to the efforts of those who, like Ralph Waldo Emerson, have sensed man's 'occult relation' with the vegetable world, there are already a dozen protected areas. Nature reservations range from luxuriant *lövängar*, such as Ramsholmen, near Mariehamn, and Idö in Kökar, through tracts of rare flora, bird sanctuaries and nesting grounds, such as Björkör in Föglö, to unusual geological formations, such as the curiously eroded granite shore of Källskär in Kökar parish. The interests of recreationist and conservationist need to be harmonised. Both point to the need for a comprehensive and integrated plan. This is especially true of the coastal areas where rights of access and restraints on access need to be balanced. At present, *allemans rätt* prevails; this freedom to go ashore whenever and wherever a man wishes is a good principle in common law, but increasingly out of joint with the times. Its implications are especially significant for the natural life of the outer skerries. Conservationists point first to the need for restrictions on access to islands where birds are nesting between 1 April and 31 July Even after that, the risk of killing chicks remains high. For certain birds, such as the grey goose and the swan, even more restrictive controls seem necessary. Curiously enough, current restraints apply only to areas in the vicinity of skerry settlements. It is true that considerably more harm is done to bird colonies by the springtime shoot (in which all Ålanders and those who own land in Åland have the right to participate) than by summer visitors, but as in so many biological fields it is the combined impact of a variety of pressures that may result in the extinction of a species. Åland's birds of prey have already virtually disappeared. Its sea mammals have long since been decimated. In the countryside, as distinct from on the sea coast, it is the pressures on a sensitive flora that raise problems—not only from trampling and picking, but from the side effects of road spraying and weed killing. Above all, because of their Baltic setting, Ålanders are concerned with its growing pollution. As a tideless inland sea with low salinity, the Baltic is more subject to the effects of pollution than the outer ocean. The delicate food chains of its marine life are more easily disrupted, especially those of the shallow inshore waters which support so many of Åland's fish. Independently of the continuous risk of large and small-scale oil pollution, the intensified ferry services inevitably disturb the inshore fisheries. Furthermore, along the narrower sounds and channels where they pass, their swell and undertow can cause physical damage to nets and shore installations. While Husö biological station may concern itself academically with the consequences of these matters, the entire conservationist issue has such broad and deep implications for Åland in particular and the Swedo-Finnish skerries in general that it calls for educational instruction and campaigns at the highest level.

THE THEME OF RENEWAL

In so far as most Ålanders live close to nature, they are conscious of renewal as a theme in their lives. In contrast to most islands which suffer the erosive effects of powerful tides and currents, Åland's shores and archipelagos emerge continuously from the waves. Around its present margins, Åland is being reborn as it was in the past. The gradual process of plant colonisation can be seen at the meeting ground of land and water. At a larger scale, it is possible to recognise the counterparts of earlier Ålands. Indeed, the skerry parish of Brändö—easternmost of the island groups and most low-lying of them—has been called 'Åland in the Litorina period'. Again, Åland renews itself each spring more strikingly than anything witnessed in the more maritime parts of western Europe. The transformation of the boreal into the maritime, of imprisoning ice into open water, is a phenomenon which repeats annually the release from the Ice Age.

It will be equally clear that renewal is also written in the history of Åland. The intermittent threat of obliteration through invasion has been met by withdrawal and return. The tourist invasion is a new experience. It is a peaceful invasion and is a major new source of wealth; but, because it is not possible to withdraw from it, much that is traditional in Åland is challenged. It is arguable that the intrusion is a short-period summer experience and that the islanders are able to retreat into the winter in order to recover from the seasonal disturbance. But the new source of wealth has bred a corresponding dependence. It has also engendered new practices. It is a pleasing irony, for example, that Ålanders have succumbed to the posters of Mariehamn's tourist agencies and, like the rest of the Scandinavians, have yielded to the call of other islands. The Balearics, the Canaries, the isles of Greece—even the Caribbean and the Pacific—are within the reach of their purses. Little could Daniel Backman have dreamt, when he christened the Åland Islands the 'Bothnian Cyclades', that his descendants would come to regard a visit to their classical counterparts as a perfectly normal part of their personal experience.

The summer invasion has prompted a variety of reactions which represent a renewal of thought and action in their own right. It has stimulated a new sense of involvement which has encouraged an increasing number of Ålanders to lift their sights to a higher level. For example, it has been suggested that Åland would make an appropriate setting for a *skärgårds* institute, a more broadly based Baltic Institute for hydrological and hydro-biological research, or (through the Nordic Council) a centre for the study of environmental problems. Åland could fittingly accommodate such an organisation and its citizens have their own contribution to make to it. Though they may be less aware of the marginal circumstances of economic life than in former times, they retain an intimate concern for the detail of physical circumstances. Living close to nature they are almost unconsciously nurtured in the art of observation. Its accompaniments are a sense of detail and a sense of realism.

Biologically, economically and socially, the Åland Islands are experiencing the effects of changes that have already transformed metropolitan Sweden and Finland. A way of life which has been closely tied to the natural world is intruded upon increasingly by different, more powerful and urban-centred systems. The task is to maintain a balance between the limiting elements of the domestic situation and the limitless consequences of submission to a system of external controls. Today, the Åland Islands can live in many more different ways than in former times. Equally, they can die many more different deaths. The objective is a living *skärgård* which is something more than a museum piece. The *skärgård* must change, but the nature and degree of change must be controlled. Åland is faced with the problem of creating and maintaining an organisation which is capable of keeping its land healthy in body and its people healthy in mind. On balance, the Åland Isles remain fortunate isles—*Fortunatorum insulae*. Ålanders are aware of the broader range of choices presented to them. Less clear to them are the consequences of the decisions that must be taken when they are faced with situations which are not just old destinies dressed in new disguises.

AFTERWORD

THIS book has its origins in three field excursions in which we shared. In 1959, in the company of the late Helmer Smeds, we took a party of Finnish undergraduates on a tour through Åbo and Åland archipelagos. The tour was by way of preparation for an excursion arranged for the Stockholm Congress of the International Geographical Union in 1960. In 1963, we organised a study visit to Åland for the Geographical Field Group. The visit was based on Saltvik and a report based on the contributions of the thirty participants is listed in the bibliography.

Most of the publications used in preparing this book are in Swedish; they are given as a bibliography. The largest collection of literature about Åland (*Alandica samling*) is in the library of Åbo Åkademi. There are also collections in Mariehamn's public library and in Ålands Bank, Mariehamn. Ålands sjöfartsmuseum has a library devoted to sea-going and a large number of ships' logbooks. Administrative records for all the principal agencies of the provincial government are kept in Mariehamn. In Finland, the registration of births, marriages and deaths are the responsibility of the church, so that each Ålandic vicarage has its own archive.

Ålanders are Swedish-speaking, but because Finland is officially bilingual Finnish as well as Swedish place names are given in the index and, for the first time of use, in the text. Most of the places to which reference is made can be found on the Åland 1: 100,000 sheet of the Finnish Topographical Survey. Åland is also covered by maps on a scale 1: 20,000, sheets of which are available from *Lantmäteristyrelsen,* Helsinki (*Maanmittaushallitus,* Helsinki). *Lantmäteristyrelsen* also has a rich collection of early taxation and land reorganisation maps. *The Atlas of the Archipelago of south-western Finland* (Helsinki, 1960) devotes about half its space to the Åland archipelago. *Ålands skärgård, sjökort in miniatyrformat* (Helsinki, 1959) provides detailed nautical information.

It is a measure of the concern of Ålanders for the conservation of their landscape that they have sponsored a landscape classification map and text for the whole of their territory. It is the work of Håkan Kulves: *Planeringsrådet i Landskapet Åland,* 16 vols (Mariehamn, 1974).

BIBLIOGRAPHY

ACERBI, JOSEPH. *Travels to the North Cape.* London, 1802
AHLBÄCK, RAGNA. *Kökar, Folklivs Studier.* IV. Helsinki, 1955
ANDERSSON, SVEN. 'Oståländska skärgården under kriget 1808–9', *Budkaveln* (1945)
ARNELL, SIGRID. *Illustrated Moss Flora of Fennoscandia,* I. 1954
Atlas of the Archipelago of South-western Finland and Text. Nordenskiöld Society, Helsinki, 1960
BARROS, JAMES. *The Åland Islands Question: Its Settlement by the League of Nations.* London, 1968
BERGQUIST, N. O. *Lumparen, Hav eller Bygd?* Ekenäs, 1959
BLOMFELT, FRANK. *Åländska Emigrationen 1856–1918.* Mariehamn, 1965
BLOMQVIST, ANNI. *I Stormens Spår.* Tammerfors, 1967
——. *Vägen till Stormskäret.* Tammerfors, 1968
——. *Maja.* Borgå, 1970
——. *I kamp med havet.* Helsinki, 1971
——. *Vägen från Stormskäret.* Helsinki, 1973
BONDESTAM, ANNA. *Åland Vintern 1918.* Mariehamn, 1972
CLARKE, E. D. *Travels in various countries of Europe.* London 1823, III
DERBY, W. L. A. *The Tall Ships Pass.* London, 1937
DOLBEY, E. T. *Sketches in the Baltic.* London, 1854
DONNER, OSSIAN. *Åtta år. Memoir anteckningar, 1918–26.* Oxford, 1927
DREIJER, MATTS. 'Det återfunna Birka', *Åländsk Odling* (1969), 3–35
——. *Häuptlinge, Kaufleute und Missionare im Norden vor tausend Jahren.* Åbo, 1960
—— (ed). *Mariehamn stadshistoria, 1911–61.* Helsinki, 1962
——. 'Problem i Nordenmissionshistoria', *Åländsk Odling* (1965), 3–24
——. *Redernas ömsesidiga försäkringsbolag, 1938–68.* Mariehamn, 1969
DREIJER, STIG. *Åland under stora nordiska kriget.* Mariehamn, 1970
ERIKSSON, PAMELA. *The Duchess.* London, 1959
FAGERLUND, L. W. 'Anteckningar rörande samfärdseln emellan

Sverige och Finland öfver Ålands haf och de åländska öarna', *Åland*, VIII. Helsinki, 1925

GARDBERG, JOHN. 'Torskmärken kring Möskär och Kökarsören', *Budkaveln* (1964–5), 158–92

——. 'En drängs dagbok från Seglinge', *Budkaveln* (1946), 97–116 *Glimtar över Åland*, Åbo, 1942

GREITZ, BJÖRN, and STENMARK, ANDERS. *Det Ålandska Undret*. Stockholm, 1973

GRÜSSNER, A. J. *Die Ålands-Inseln im Ostseeraum*. Bremen, 1937

HAUSEN, H. 'De gamla strandbildningarna på Åland och deras förhållande till stenåldersboplatserna', *Fennia*, 28, 3 (1910)

——. *Geologisk Beskrivning över Landskapet Åland*. Mariehamn, 1964

——. 'Groundwater in the Åland *rapakivi* massif', *Terra*, 85, 2 (1973)

——. 'Orografiska studier på Åland med särskild hänsyn till rapakivi berggrunden och dess förklyftnings-förhållanden', *Fennia*, 28, 4 (1910)

—— (ed). *Ålands Natur*. Åbo, 1948

HEDENSTIERNA, BERTIL. 'Stockholms skärgård', *Geografiska Annaler*, 30 (Stockholm, 1948)

HINZE, BERTIL. *Karl Emanuel Jansson, en åländsk Malare*. Helsinki, 1924

HIRN, MARTA. *Från Bomarsund till Sveaborg*, 1854–55, Helsinki, 1956

HORNBORG, EIRIK (ed). *En spanare under stora ofreden, Stefan Löfvings dagbok över hans äventyr i Finland och Sverige*, 1710–20, Helsinki

HUGHES, J. W. *Two Summer Cruises in the Baltic*. London, 1856

HUSTICH, ILMARI. *Finlands skärgård*. Borgå, 1964

ISACHSSON, M. 'Ägoförhållanden i Frebbenby', *Åländsk Odling* (1967), 38–40

JAATINEN, STIG. *Bidrag till kännedom om de ålandska sjöarnas strandvegetation*. Helsinki, 1950

——. *Regional drag i befolkningsutvecklingen på Åland*, *1900–50*. Helsinki, 1953

——. 'De senaste decenniernas befolknings—och näringsgeografiska utveckling på Åland', *Terra* (1954), 2

——. 'Archipelagoes in comparison. Outer Hebrides and the Åland Islands', *Acta Geographica*, 16 (Helsinki, 1957)

——. 'The glacial morphology of Åland, with special reference to the Quaternary deposits', *Fennia*, 84, 1 (1960)

——. 'Expansion and retreat of settlement in the southwestern archipelago of Finland', *Fennia*, 84, 2 (1960)

BIBLIOGRAPHY

JAATINEN, STIG. 'Geografisk regionplanering på Åland', *Åländsk Odling* (1968)

——. 'Mariehamns befolkning', *Åländsk Odling* (1962)

JANSSON, GERD, 'Trolldomsprocesserna på Åland', *Åländsk Odling* (1970), 156–76

KARLING, STEN. *Ålands medeltida Kyrkor*. Stockholm, 1973

KARLSSON, ELIS. *Mother Sea*. Oxford, 1964

——. *Pulley-Haul*. London, 1966

KERKKONEN, GUNVOR. *Bondesegel på Finska viken*. Helsinki, 1959

—— (ed). *Åländska Handlingar, 1530–1634*, II, 4

——. *Ålands silverskatteregister, 1571*. Mariehamn, 1965

KING, CUCHLAINE, and HIRST, RACHEL. 'The Boulder Fields of the Åland Islands', *Fennia*, 89, 2 (1963)

KIRBY, W. F. *Kalevala*. London, 1961, 1966

KIVIKOSKI, Ella. *Finland* (Ancient Peoples and Places). London 1967

——. *Kvarnbacken, Ein Gräbenfeld der jüngeren Eisenzeit auf Åland*. Helsinki, 1963

——. 'Problem rörande Ålands Järnåldersbebyggelse', *Soc Sc Fennica Årsbok*, XL, 5 (1962)

KULVES, HÅKAN, and HARBERG, GÖRAN. *Skärgård, Sammanbrott eller Utveckling*. Borgå, 1971

KÅHRE, GEORG. *Den Åländska Segelsjöfartens Historia*. Helsinki, 1940

——. *Under Gustaf Eriksons Flagga*. Mariehamn, 1948

La Question des Iles d'Åland. Helsinki, 1920

LÉOUZON LE DUC, L. *Les Iles d'Åland*. Paris, 1854

LINDQUIST, IVAR. 'Ålands runinskrift, Sund Korset', *Åländsk Odling* (1969), 36–51

LUNDQUIST, BO. 'De åländska prästerskapets ekonomiska förhållanden under 1600 och 1700 talen', *Åländsk Odling* (1961), 126–68

——. 'Midsommarstängerna i Finland', *Suomen Museo* (1971)

MAGOUN, FRANCIS PEABODY JR. *Kalevala*. Cambridge, Mass, 1963

MANNERHEIM, C. G. *The Memoirs of Marshal Mannerheim*. London, 1953

——. *Människa och miljö i Finlands skärgård* (Nordenskiöld Samfundet) Helsinki, 1974

——. *Mariehamns stads historia, 1911–61* (Stadsstyrelsen i Mariehamn) Mariehamn, 1962

MEAD, W. R. *Finland*, (How People Live). London, 1965 (chapter on Kökar)

——. *Saltvik, Studies from an Åland Parish*. Nottingham, 1964

——. 'The Conquest of Finland', *The Norseman*, IX, i, 2 (1951)

BIBLIOGRAPHY

MEAD, W. R. and SMEDS, HELMER. *Finland in Winter*. London, 1967

MIKANDER, KAJ (ed). *Skatteböcker, 1557–1639*. Mariehamn, 1964

——. *Åländska Handlingar, 1530–1634*, II, I

——. *Jordeböcker, 1557–1605*. Mariehamn, 1969

MODEEN, TORE. *Om de folkrättligar garantierna för bevarandet av Ålandsöarnas nationella Karaktär*. Ekenäs, 1965

MORENIUS, BOETIUS. *Acta visitatoria, 1637–66*. Borgå, 1908

MÖRN, YNGVE. *Fiske och Fiskehamnar på Åland*. Mariehamn, 1971

'Naturvårdsproblem i skärgården', *Husö Biologiska Station*, 15 (Mariehamn, 1971)

NORDBERG, KARL. *En öst-Åländsk skärgårdsby, Lappo i Brändö*. Åbo, 1925

NYMAN, VALDEMAR. 'De unggotiska målningarna i Lemlands kyrka', *Åländsk Odling* (1958), 3–49

——. *Den stora flykten*. Helsinki, 1953

——. 'Medeltidsmålningarna i Finström St. Michael', *Åländsk Odling* (1964), 28–58

——. *Längs åländska vägar*, Borgå, 1963

——. 'Pastor i Finströms vattenrätt och fisketionde', *Åländsk Odling* (1957), 65–102

——. *Åland, midsommarstångens land*. Helsinki, 1955

OTTER, WILLIAM. *The Life and Remains of E. D. Clarke*. London, 1824

PALMGREN, A. *Studier över löfängsområdena på Åland*. Helsinki, 1915

——. *Studier över havsstrandens vegetation och flora på Åland*. Helsinki, 1961

PAPP, DAVID. *Åländsk allmogeseglation, 1800–1940*. Mariehamn, 1971

PIPPING, K., and PIPPING-VAN HULTEN, I. *Den åländska ungdomens emigration*. Mariehamn, 1961

PYE, PETER. *A sail in the forest*. London, 1961

RADLOFF, FREDRIC WILHELM. *Beskrifning öfver Åland*. Åbo, 1795

ROOS, JOHN E. (ed). *John Stiernhööks åländska domböcker, 1641–3*, Mariehamn, 1946

Russian War, 1854, Baltic; 1855, Baltic Official Correspondence (Navy Society), London, 1943, 1944

ROSLIN, B. *Åland i ett regional-ekonomiskt perspektiv*. Mariehamn, 1973

SALMINEN, SALLY. *Barndomens land*. Helsinki, 1948

——. *Katrina*. New York, 1937

——. *Upptäcktsresan*. Helsinki, 1966

SALONEN, KRISTER. *Det åländska jordbruket och dess binäringar*, Mariehamn, 1970

BIBLIOGRAPHY

SCHEVELIN-MALMSTRÖM, U. S. 'Folkelig läkekonst på Åland', *Åländsk Odling* (1967), 121–33

SJÖBLOM, WALTER. *Mariehamns stads historia, 1861–1911.* Mariehamn, 1911

SKULT, H. 'Skogsbotaniska studier i skärgårdshavet', *Acta Botanica Fennica,* 57 (1956)

Skärgårdsboken. (Nordenskiöld Society), Helsinki, 1948

STORMBOM, JARL. 'Om det åländska båtmånshallet', *Åländsk Odling* (1956), 32–74

SUNDWALL, JOHANNES (ed). *Ålands medeltidsurkunder,* I. Helsinki, 1954

Sveriges krig åren 1808–09, Pt IV. Stockholm, 1905

TALLQVIST, GÖSTA. *En bok om Åland.* Helsinki, 1910

TAPSELL, ALAN. *Northward but gently.* Stockholm, 1969

TOPELIUS, ZACHRIS. *Samlade skrifter,* V. Helsinki, 1920

TÄRNSTRÖM, CHRISTOPHERUS. *De Ålandia maris Baltici insula.* Uppsala, 1739

TÖRNROOS, BIRGER. *Båtar och båtbyggare i Ålands östra skärgård.* Åbo, 1968

Utvecklingsdelegationen för landskapet Åland, betänkande, I, II. Mariehamn, 1971

WAHLBÄCK, KRISTER. *Finlandsfrågen i svensk politik 1937–40.* Stockholm, 1964

WECKSTRÖM, M. *Åland, geografiska-statistiska Lexikon över Finland.* Åbo, 1852

WESTERHOLM, GRETA. *I sommarhatt till Åland.* Åbo, 1940

WESTERMARCK, E. *Memoirs of my Life.* London, 1929

Ålands folkmusik för två fioler, 6 vols. Stockholm, 1956–8

Ålandsfrågan inför Nationernas Förbund, 3 vols. Stockholm, 1920–1

Ålands självstyrelse 25 år. Stockholm, 1947

Ålands skärgård, sjökort i miniatyrformat. Helsinki, 1959 (Corrections are published in the three-monthly Notices to Mariners for Sweden and Finland)

Ålänningarna och deras näringsliv. Mariehamn, 1969

INDEX

Acerbi, Joseph, 79
Administration, 89, 135-7, 167
Af Schultén, Nathaniel, 140
Ahlbäck, Ragna, 74
Alcohol, 134
Alexander II, 23, 88; III, 164
Ancylus Lake, 30, 40
Ansgar, Bishop of Bremen, 66
Antiquities, 11
Autonomy law, 19, 109, 134
Åbo (F. Turku), 73, 74, 86, 87, 88, 128, 139, 142, 145; Akademi, 140, 172; archipelago, 11, 37; Peace of, 95
Ängskärsfjärden, 28

Backman, Daniel, 170
Bertby, 93
Birds, 55, 60-1, 83, 168-9
Birka, 66-7
Blomqvist, Anni, 154
Bogskär, 140
Bomarsund, 18, 21, 97-103, 155, 164
Borgå (F. Porvoo), 96
Brierly, Oswald, 100
Britain, 86, 87, 97-103
Bronze Age, 64
Bryce, Lord, 106-7
Brändö, 16, 28, 50, 70, 93, 96, 114, 118, 122, 127, 139, 148, 159 169,
Bus services, 127

Camping, 165, 167
Carr, Sir John, 80

Carrying trade, 85-7
Cattle, 68, 77, 78, 80, 82, 113, 116
Census, 79
Charts, 140
Christianity, 66-7
Christmas, 84, 161
Church: paintings, 70; registers, 131; structure, 68, 94, 103, 155, 163
Clarke, E. D., 79-80
Climate, 14-15, 39-47, 98-9, 114, 116
Communications, 118, 136; air, 128; bridges, 127; footpaths, 128; roads, 123-8
Conservation, 57, 167-8
Cooperative organisations, 119, 122, 136, 153
Crayfish, 148-9, 164
Crofters (torpare), 85
Curzon, Lord, 106
Customs, 160-4
Cycling, 127

Dahlberg, Erik, 18, 69
Dardel, F. L. von, 102
Degerby, 142
Demilitarisation, 102, 109-11
Depopulation, 134
Dolby, E. T., 102
Drainage: artificial, 119, 120, 128; natural, 37-8, 59
Drumlins, 30
Döbeln, General von, 96

179

Eckerö, 16, 27, 54, 57, 85, 93, 141–2, 146, 163
Education, 77, 91, 128, 135
Electricity, 119, 120, 123
Emigration, 112, 122, 129–34, 159
Employment, 116, 131, 156
Enclosure movement (*storskifte*), 78
Engel, C. F., 141
Eric XIV, 69
Erikson, Gustav, 108, 149–53, 156–7
Eriksson, Pamela, 87, 149
Ethnography, 19, 160–4

Farm: associations, 91, 136; buildings, 117, 120–1; crops, 113–14; houses; 120–2; labour, 119–20; mechanisation, 78; ownership, 113, 133; rationalisation, 117; reorganisation, 78; specialisation, 117
Farming, 76, 77, 80–1, 82, 87, 112–22, 133, 136; fur, 118, 147
Fauna, 59–61, 168–9
Ferries, 11–12, 46, 123–7, 136, 138–9, 141, 145–6, 153, 169
Finström, 16, 57, 68, 88, 95, 104, 135; church, 17, 69, 70, 90, 94
Fish, 37, 51; cultivation, 148; processing, 122, 147, 169
Fishing, 47, 80, 83, 145, 146–9; fleet, 139, 146
Flag, 23, 164
Floating dock, 156
Flora, 14, 48–62, 168–9
Folk: costumes, 160; dancing, 160; high school, 91; lore, 16, 102
Food, 83, 84, 163
Forestry, 116
France, 86, 97–103
Fredrikshamn (F. Hamina), Treaty of, 96
Fuel, 99, 123, 139
Fungi, 58, 84, 120
Föglö, 16, 22, 93, 122, 127, 148, 154, 159, 168

Geology, 26–33
Germany, 86, 104–6, 110–11
Geta, 16, 31, 38, 57, 66, 93, 96
Getaberg, 31, 128, 132
Glaciation, 14, 29–31, 39–40
Godby, 88, 105
Gotland, 48, 56, 68, 70
'Grain race', 150–2
Granberg, J. P., 41
Granit, Alfons, 104
Greenhouses, 117
Grelsby, 69, 104
Grisslehamn, 92, 96, 129, 139, 146
Gustaf Adolf IV, 22, 95
Gustav III, 22, 99
Gustavs (F. Kustavi), 139
Gustavus Vasa, 69

Haga, 38, 69
Hammarland, 16, 27, 29, 31, 32, 57, 65, 76, 96, 122, 123, 147, 163
Helsinki, 74, 141, 147
Herring, 51, 107, 147
Hornborg, Eirik, 33
Horticulture, 117–18
Hotels, 164–5, 167
Housing, 87–8, 120–2, 136
Hughes, Rev J. W., 100–1
Hultaberget, 128
Husö biological station, 169

Ice boat, 145
Icebreakers, 108, 145
Idö, 168
Immigration, 109, 134
Ingman, Matti, 156
Insurance, 87
Iron Age, 64–5
Iron ore, 29, 123

Jansson, K. E., 35, 85
Johansson, A. W., 41
Jomala, 16, 29, 31, 32, 64, 68, 70, 88, 95, 135, 156, 163; church, 69; farm research station, 118

Kalevala, 65
Karlsson, Elis, 76, 151
Kasberget, 128
Kastelholm, 18, 21, 69, 70, 72, 97, 163
Klang, Roland, 160
Kulves, Håkan, 33
Kumlinge, 16, 69, 78, 93, 96, 114, 115, 127, 128, 132, 136, 139, 148, 159
Kyrksund, 28, 59
Källskär, 33, 168
Käringsund, 54, 147
Kökar, 16, 33, 50, 57, 64, 65, 68, 83, 88, 114, 127, 132, 139, 147, 148, 153, 159, 168

Labour supply, 122–3, 136
Lakes, 59
Land: reclamation, 120; registers, 73; uplift, 31–2, 38, 48, 59, 169; use, 114–17
Language, 19, 109, 162, 172
League of Nations, 21, 106–10, 133
Ledsund, 93, 100; battle of, 94–5
Legal structure, 70
Lemland, 16, 32, 38, 57, 59, 65, 69, 85, 86, 87, 88, 93, 95, 136, 167
Léouzon le Duc, L., 19, 80, 120
Lichens, 52–3
Lighthouses, 140–1
Limestone, 28–9, 123
Linnaeus, Carl, 22, 26
Litorina Sea, 31, 40, 169
Logbooks, 85, 98, 150
Lucia, 161
Lumparen Bay, 29, 38, 97, 103, 120
Lumparland, 10
Långnäs, 139
Löving, Stefan, 93
Lövångar, 56–7, 70, 88, 168

Malthus, Thomas, 79, 80
Mannerheim, Marshal, 105
Manufacturing industry, 122–3

Maps, 76, 78, 95
Mariehamn (F. Maarianhamina), 12–13, 23–4, 37, 41, 42, 64, 88, 89, 103, 110, 113, 123, 124, 126, 128, 129, 132, 134, 142, 145, 149, 151, 165, 168, 172
Martha Society, 163–4
Medical services, 78, 84, 128, 135
Mercantile marine, 85, 111, 139, 142–6
Meteorological observations, 41
Midsummer pole, 143, 161–2
Modeen, Tore, 111
Monastic foundations, 68
Morenius, Boetus, 77
Motor vehicles, 124–5
Museums: maritime, 143, 152, 163; Åland, 163; Jan Karlsgård, 163; local, 163
Märket, 14, 41

Napier, Admiral Sir Charles, 98, 102–3
Naval commitment, 75–6, 95, 96
Navigation, 86, 140–1; aids, 140–1; school, 138
Newby, Eric, 151
Newspapers, 23, 113, 129
Nordenskiöld, Adolf Erik, 22, 145
Nordic Council, 23, 113, 170; labour market, 134
Nyhamn, 29, 123
Nyman, Valdemar, 93, 157, 160
Nystad (F. Uusikaupunki), 129, 145, 156; Treaty of, 94

Orrdalsklint, 31, 128

Palmgren, Alvar, 30
Peatland, 32, 59
Peter the Great, 22, 93
Peterson, Johannes, 73
Pilots, 79, 95, 98, 139
Place names, 67, 172
Plebiscite, 106

INDEX

Pollution, 38, 154, 169
Pommern, 13, 24, 108, 150, 152
Population, 79; mobility, 129–33;
  registration, 130; structure, 131–2
Porter, Sir Robert Ker, 79–80
Post route, 21, 79–80, 92–3, 104,
  123, 124, 146
Prehistory, 63–7
Property laws, 167
Prästö, 103

Radio, 129
Radloff, F. W., 41, 78–9, 92
Ramsholmen, 30, 57, 168
Rapakivi, 26–9, 38, 55
Research institutes, 118, 169, 170
Rune stones, 66–7
Russia, 21, 78, 85, 92–105, 110–11,
  141, 154, 164

Sailing fleet, 149–57
St Petersburg, 22, 97, 98, 133, 142,
  165
Salminen, Sally, 103, 114, 150
Salmon, 148
Saltvik, 16, 30, 31, 65–6, 68, 76, 77,
  114, 156, 163, 172
Sandstones, 28–9
Sealing, 80, 83
Seals, 60, 148
Seglinge, 80
Shipping, 24, 138–57; agents, 156;
  repairs, 156
Shipwrecks, 153–4
Shooting, 164
Signildskär, 22, 68, 96, 141, 145
Simskäla, 36, 134
Sjöberg, Valentin, 111
Skarpans, 97, 103, 156
Skiftet, 11, 109, 167
Skiöldebrand, A. F., 111
Smuggling, 134–5
Soils, 31–2, 114
Sonck, Lars, 103
Sottunga, 16, 22, 96, 127, 159

Stockholm, 74, 80, 86, 88, 102, 128,
  139, 141, 142, 145, 147, 168;
  archipelago, 11, 88, 159, 160
Stone Age, 31, 63–4
Subsidisation, 130, 135, 142
Sund, 16, 28, 30, 64, 67, 93, 97, 127,
  148; church, 69
Sundblom, Julius, 104, 143
Sveaborg (F. Suomenlinna), 97
Sälskär, 41, 67, 140

Tallquist, Gösta, 91
Telephone, 129
Television, 122, 129
Timber industry, 81, 90, 116
Tin, 29
Tithe, 73
Topelius, Zachris, 24, 26, 69, 160
Tourism, 22, 112, 135–7, 148, 156,
  158–9, 164–9, 170; numbers,
  165–6
Trawling, 107, 146–7, 148
Tärnström, Christopher, 51, 78

USA, 133

Vargata, 86, 103
Verkviken, 29
Vikings, 66
Vårdö, 16, 36, 76, 86, 93, 117, 127,
  132, 139, 154, 159

War: Åland, 97–103; Civil (1917–
  18), 104–5; Crimean, 21, 92, 97–
  103, 156; Great Northern, 92–4;
  Little Northern, 94–5; Napo-
  leonic, 92, 95–7, 141; World War
  I, 103–10, 140, 149; World War
  II, 110–11, 140, 142
Water supply, 37–8, 121, 136, 167
Wenström, Henrik August, 80
Westerholm, Greta, 88
Westermarck, Edvard, 109, 133

Windmills, 122, 163

Winter, 13, 45–7, 60, 80, 84–5, 96, 98, 108, 125, 127–8, 139, 141, 145, 170

Woodlands, 49–50, 57–8, 75, 77, 167

Yachting, 155

Yoldia Sea, 30